THE UNSEEING EYE

*The Myth of Television Power
in National Politics*

THE UNSEEING EYE

The Myth of Television Power in National Politics

by
Thomas E. Patterson
Robert D. McClure

G. P. Putnam's Sons
New York

SBN: 399-50367-6

Library of Congress Cataloging in Publication Data

Patterson, Thomas E.
   The Unseeing Eye.

   1. Television in politics—United States.
I. McClure, Robert D., joint author.   II.   Title.
HE8700.7.P6P37   1975   324'2   75-43834

*To Ellie, Mother and Dad, and
the rest of the Pattersons*

—TEP

To Barbara and Katie

—RDM

Acknowledgments

A GRANT from the National Science Foundation provided the basic support for this book. We sincerely acknowledge our gratitude.

We are indebted to a number of people for their encouragement, advice, and aid: Warren Weaver of the New York *Times,* who first showed us that others could be excited by our work and, later, wrote the book's foreword; Herbert Alexander of the Citizens' Research Foundation, who brought attention to the study by publishing a monograph of our early findings on political advertising and who constantly prodded us to keep writing; Charles Guggenheim of Guggenheim Productions, who created George McGovern's advertising campaign and warmly shared his time and thoughts with us; William Taylor of Ogilvie-Mather Advertising, who developed Richard Nixon's advertising campaign and with excitement and good humor informed us about making political spots; Gerald Kline of the department of journalism at the University of Michigan, who was our best publicist and friendliest critic; Ronald Malovsky of the National Broadcasting Company, who helped us improve our measurement of television exposure; and Martin Fishbein of the department of psychology at the University of Illinois, who, through his books and articles, provided us with the measurement techniques that give our research intellectual coherence. Anne Martindale, our editor at Putnam, deserves a most special thanks. Her enthusiasm for what we were writ-

7

ing boosted our spirits and hastened our efforts. Her editing and substantive suggestions helped our thinking and writing. No one could been more helpful or patient. We owe her much.

Among our colleagues at Syracuse University, two persons have been unusually supportive—John Hodgson, former chairman of the department of political science, and Alan K. Campbell, Dean of the Maxwell School of Citizenship and Public Affairs, both of whom made certain we had the time, facilities, and environment to do our work.

But more than anything else, the success of a survey research project depends on the prompt, accurate handling of the tedious, unending, day-to-day tasks it generates. Rick Ender, our graduate student and administrative assistant, handled these chores for more than two years. He was indispensable. More than anyone else, he is responsible for the data on which this book is based.

Without graduate students most university research could not be done. In the past three years, we were fortunate to have several of them—Jim Campbell, Guy Martin, Ken Meier, Robert Milne, and Henry Muse—who gave us more of their time and expertise than we had the right to expect.

In addition to this core group of graduate assistants, we are indebted to a platoon of undergraduate and graduate students who contributed in countless ways to the writing of this book: Bruce Baldwin, Joyce Bloom, Scott Chatfield, Steve Clendenen, Mike Connery, Tony DeBonis, Jim Fitchett, Theodore Flack, Fred Gaske, Mark Harris, David Hopkins, Henry Hovemeyer, Bob Kalik, Lois Levitan, Bill Liebman, George Lopez, Cindy Ludvigsen, Jane Moulton, Mike Nauer, Kevin Quinn, Myrna Rechtman, Jyoti Shah, Jan Tewes, Eileen Titmuss, Raymond Torello, Susan Vercillo, Lauren Watts, Michael Whack, and Joan Zubras.

We also pay tribute to our secretaries over the past three years—Leslie Henderson, Linda Lagua, Ella Pinals, Helenanne Robertson, Marilyn Rosen, and Gloria Tripolone—and those in the political science department—Rose Difasi and

June Dumas. Through draft after draft of papers, books, and interview schedules, they have typed thousands of words with accuracy and good humor. Gloria Tripolone, who painstakingly typed and otherwise contributed to the final manuscript, deserves our special thanks.

We also acknowledge our debt to the staff of more than fifty interviewers who visited the homes of the voters and viewers about whom we write. Their patience and skill in administering a challenging interview was the first step toward the completion of this book.

And finally, we want to thank the men and women we interviewed. Much of what we have to say that accurately describes television and politics, our respondents first told us. We simply listened. So whatever merits the book may have we share with them. Its errors and shortcomings are ours alone.

Preface

DESPITE TELEVISION'S expanding role in American presidential elections, its impact on the voters has not been known. Before this book, no major study had systematically examined television's influence.[1] In this regard, Herbert E. Alexander of the Citizens Research Foundation, and former director of the Presidential Commission on Campaign Costs, recently said:

> Television may influence the citizen's opinion of the electoral process itself, and may serve to either strengthen or undermine the nation's confidence in its institutions and its democracy. Yet social scientists using modern techniques have not yet really told us what we want to know about the impact of television on politics. . . . Much more is known about the effects of advertising on consumer behavior than about the impact of political communication—whether presented in news or as direct advertising—on voter behavior.[2]

This book provides what has been missing. It offers the first accurate, detailed information about many aspects of politics that have been hotly debated for the past decade or so.

In the pages that follow, we look at television's role in building a candidate's public image, in educating the electorate about critical issues and events, and in influencing how people vote. We try to provide reliable answers to two major questions: How manipulative is political television? How informative is political television?

We could not have written this book without the help of a grant from the National Science Foundation.[3] A major reason why television's impact has never been studied before is that careful research on this topic is expensive and time-consuming. The National Science Foundation's grant provided us the necessary funds to collect more than two thousand interviews with voters and to monitor closely the political content of network television news and televised political advertising during a presidential campaign. We have spent the past three years examining that material, weighing its meaning, and writing our conclusions.

Televised politics fascinates and concerns many people, and we have written this book for all of them: the politicians and campaign consultants who must use political television; the television and print journalists who wish to know more about how their actions affect the public; the average citizens who want to keep informed about the political world in which they live; the students in government and mass communication courses who, by choice or scheduling fate, expect to learn something about politics and the media; and social scientists who are concerned with political communication.

To accommodate scholars and students, we have prepared a series of technical appendices on the research methods. In the back of the book, these appendices describe the survey design used in obtaining the voter interviews which furnish much of our evidence and the content analysis of television news and advertising which provides the rest.

To accommodate other readers, we have excluded from the main text all intricate statistics and technical terms. The evidence we present is easily understandable. As simply as we can, we state what we know.

Perhaps this attempt to address a diverse audience will make everyone unhappy. Scholars may decry its imprecisions and scorn its concessions to the unwashed. Lay readers may find too much data and too much nit-picking. But we hope our book will reveal that relevant social science research can be interesting, accurate, and widely shared.

THOMAS E. PATTERSON
ROBERT D. MCCLURE
Syracuse, New York
September, 1975

Contents

Foreword

by Warren Weaver, Jr.

DURING nine months of the 1972 national political campaign, I watched television for the New York *Times*. I persuaded the editors of the paper, where I had worked since 1948, that we had previously been covering the false campaign—staged events and synthetic crowds—and that the real campaign was observable in the media. My thesis was that voters base their choices on what they read in the newspapers, hear on radio and watch on television, that it was in this composite arena that the winners actually won and the losers lost.

The concept did not originate with me, but no news-gathering agency had ever tried to cover a campaign this way before. Convinced in advance of the awesome power of broadcast political commercials, I locked myself in a series of motel rooms from Manchester, New Hampshire, to Los Angeles, turned on the television and my transistor radio and attempted to tell our readers the various ways the candidates were trying to solicit their favor during the presidential primaries.

Groping my way through largely unexplored territory, I did not expand my coverage to include the amount and character of attention given the candidates in broadcast news programs until the primaries were over. Accepting the pervasive newspaper view that our broadcast colleagues held the real levers of power, I did not attempt to examine print media impact until the general election. But, overall, I did tell the *Times* readers a good deal about how the candidates were attempting to manipulate them and what techniques seemed more or less successful.

Now, three years later, come Tom Patterson and Bob McClure, a pair of audacious young academics, to tell me that practically everything I did in 1972 was wrong. If their survey underlying this remarkable book is accurate—and since no one has ever tried this before, there is no contradictory evidence—the common assumptions by candidates, politicians and reporters about the political impact of the media are almost all 180 degrees off target. For me, the only saving grace is that Patterson and McClure were just as ignorant of this in 1972 as I was.

If this pioneering book does not send shock waves through the broadcasting industry, the major political strategists of both parties, the political science community and the professional campaign managers, nothing ever will. Consider just a few of the startling claims that the authors document:

• Political commercials, considered a devastating weapon since 1964, have almost no power to overcome a voter's preexisting view of a candidate and his party.

• These television spots, scorned by the intelligentsia as too short and gimmicky to provide an honest basis for political choice, actually furnish voters with a great deal of serious issue information.

• Television news coverage of the campaign, long touted for its impact, was no more influential than newspaper coverage in affecting the voters' views of the candidates.

Patterson and McClure combine these highly controversial conclusions with a devastating attack on the television networks' coverage of the 1972 campaign, an indictment so carefully drafted and supported that it is bound to have repercussions in the board rooms of the broadcast industry and, one devoutly hopes, affect the way television approaches the 1976 primaries and general election.

After auditing and analyzing every evening news program

on the three major networks during the general election, the authors could find very little information about the candidates' issue positions or qualifications but a great deal about rallies, motorcades, crowds, polls and other superficial aspects of the presidential election. When Patterson and McClure charge that the networks "are failing to live up to the media's traditional responsibility to keep the public politically informed," they have the figures to prove it.

Having been offered this forum, however, I would like to record a mild demurrer or two. I think the authors have a tendency to ignore the fact that campaign trivia on the news shows was frequently identified as just that. The transcript they quote of a televised Nixon visit to Atlanta makes it perfectly clear to the viewers that this was a stage-managed event. Again I remember fondly a piece by Cassie Mackin of NBC during the hectic Florida primary that consisted of nothing but pictures of silly things candidates were doing in the morning to get on the evening news. Perhaps the public would have been better served if these reports and many others had been replaced with material on issues and candidate qualifications, but at least the networks were not allowing the politicians to fool the people.

I also regret keenly that the survey was not expanded to include political "specials" broadcast by the networks outside the evening news format. The authors make the point that the audiences for such programs are much smaller and their impact accordingly diminished, but it would have been interesting to learn how they rated on solid content and visual trivia.

It was certainly comforting, however, to learn here that regular readers of newspapers during the campaign became a good deal better informed as it progressed than regular television viewers who did not read the papers. The authors' simple statistic—that the script of a thirty-minute television news show would fit on a single newspaper page with room to spare—is one the print media would like to see more widely recognized.

Finally, it is disturbing to contemplate the possibility raised by Patterson and McClure that television news shares the responsibility with Watergate for the low esteem in which the practitioners of politics find themselves today. The version of campaigning that dominates the nation's screens, as demonstrated in this book, is one that denigrates the electoral process and discourages participation in it. By clinging stubbornly to campaign coverage that focuses on surface visual aspects of a serious and complex emotional and intellectual exercise, the networks may have encouraged the numbing negativism that clouds public life today.

In any event, those of us in the political and communications businesses owe a kingsize debt of gratitude to the authors. Subsequent studies on a larger scale using different techniques may alter their conclusions, but meanwhile they have opened our eyes to some radical new ideas.

Washington, D.C.
November, 1975

Introduction: The Mistaken View of Televised Politics

> Most informed people think television's impact is profound, and there is no question that political strategists and political candidates increasingly mold their campaigns around the use of television . . . [*and yet*] *we have no accurate measure of the impact of television on voters.*[1]
>
> —*Twentieth Century Fund Commission on Campaign Costs in the Electronic Era*

IN ALMOST every instance, the prevailing view of television's role in American presidential elections is wrong.

Politicians, journalists, academics, and gadflies have argued frequently and passionately that television news and advertising have a wide-ranging influence on voters. Since the medium presents such an intimate look at candidates and campaign events, it has been claimed that television creates the images people have of candidates, presents a particularly authentic picture of politics, has a capacity for giving the electorate unique insights about politics, and can be used to manipulate unsuspecting voters. Indeed, in most accounts, television is thought to be the most powerful medium available for persuading and communicating with the electorate.[2]

Despite the certitude with which these beliefs are held, they are inaccurate. The facts about televised presidential campaigns are these:[3]

The nightly network newscasts of ABC, CBS, and NBC present a distorted picture of a presidential election campaign. These newscasts pay only limited attention to major election issues. These newscasts almost entirely avoid discussion of the candidates' qualifications for the presidency. In-

21

stead of these serious matters, ABC, CBS, and NBC devote most of their election coverage to the trivia of political campaigning that make for flashy pictures. Hecklers, crowds, motorcades, balloons, rallies, and gossip—these are the regular subjects of network campaign stories.

Consequently, steady viewers of the nightly network newscasts learn almost nothing of importance about a presidential election. For example, people do not gain a greater knowledge of the candidates' positions on the issues from watching television news. Although the mass media have an obligation to keep the electorate informed, television news does not do so. The evening newscasts of ABC, CBS, and NBC are vastly overrated sources of basic political information.

Some people might claim that television news was never thought to be a great communicator of ideas and information, that its power is the ability to transmit images—to make candidates warm and appealing as persons to an electorate that responds to personality. But in fact, television network news is no better at transmitting images than it is at transmitting information. If fails for two reasons. First, the voter is not the fool that image politics assumes him to be. The public does not evaluate presidential candidates on their personal looks or skills as entertainers, but on their political records, which the networks fail to communicate. Second, the medium is not the message. The viewer furnishes the message. When the viewer is watching the candidate he prefers, the televised image is a good one. When watching the opposing candidate, the viewer receives a poor image.

The only noticeable effect of network campaign news is an increased tendency among voters to view politics in the same trivial terms that the newscasts depict it. Regular viewers of network news are likely to describe an election campaign as a lot of nonsense rather than a choice between fundamental issues.

As with television news, most speculation about televised political advertising has been mistaken. Despite the skilled propaganda techniques employed, advertising is not effective in manipulating voters. People are not taken in by advertising hyperbole and imagery. Just like network news and for the same reasons, exposure to televised ads has no effect on voters' images of the candidates.

But people do come to understand better where the candidates stand on election issues from watching televised political commercials. Although commercials are surely full of their own nonsense, blatant exaggerations, and superficial symbolism, presidential candidates do make heavy use of hard issue information in their advertising appeals. In fact, during the short period of the general election campaign, presidential ads contain substantially more issue content than network newscasts. This information is particularly valuable to people who pay little attention to the newspaper. Advertising serves to make these poorly informed people substantially more knowledgeable. And importantly, the information they receive through political ads serves their own self-interest better than it does the candidate's manipulative interest. They use the information to decide which candidate will do better by them, even though this may mean voting against the candidate whose advertising furnished their information. To put it bluntly, spot political commercials educate rather than hoodwink the voters.

These, then, are the real effects of television on American presidential politics. But what makes these conclusions correct? And why have so many people misjudged televised politics? The weakness of prevailing opinions is that they are the product of armchair speculation. The results of such speculation have been imaginative, frequently frightening, and seemingly plausible. But they were only guesses, and as it happens, they were wrong guesses. The novel observations presented here are not guesswork. They are the result of an encompassing research effort to assess systematically television's impact on American voters. It is the first research of its kind.

The themes of this book are based on two sources of painstakingly collected evidence. One source is the approximately two thousand hour-long personal interviews conducted with voters during the 1972 campaign. These interviews provided information about people's use of television and its effect on their thinking. These interviews were obtained in a *panel* survey, which means, simply, that the same people were contacted more than once. The same people were interviewed at the start, in the middle, and at the end of the 1972 general election campaign. As a result of this procedure, an accurate chronicle was obtained of how their thinking about the candidates and issues changed during the campaign, and what influence television played in these changes.

The second source of evidence is a content analysis of *every* political news report telecast by ABC, CBS, and NBC on their evening newscast and *every* televised political commercial shown by the candidates during the 1972 general election. Each of these news reports and political ads was examined for its manner of presentation and for what it said about the campaign, the issues, and the candidates. This analysis provides a precise accounting of how television presents a presidential campaign.

This hard evidence shows the electorate has not been manipulated by televised politics. But neither have voters benefited very much. Because the candidates believe their televised images are the key to their electoral strategy and the networks think the viewing audience is interested only in pictures of campaign hoopla, television has failed its promise to raise the quality of political debate.

Part I

NETWORK EVENING NEWS AND
THE PRESIDENTIAL CAMPAIGN:
HORSE RACE AND HOOPLA

Chapter 1
Network Evening News Coverage of a Presidential Campaign

"All You Need to Know."
> —*Advertisement for NBC evening news*

"That's tonight's news."
> —*Closing comment on ABC evening news*

"And that's the way it is."
> —*Walter Cronkite's closing comment on the CBS evening news*

IN its coverage of a presidential campaign, network news frequently places exciting pictures ahead of informative reporting. The nightly newscasts of ABC, CBS, and NBC often ignore the substance of election politics to concentrate on the trivial, but colorful, campaign shenanigans that provide good film.

One October day in the 1972 campaign, for instance, George McGovern delivered an important speech in New York City. Billed as the Democratic candidate's law and order speech, his statement contained comprehensive plans for dealing with crime in America. McGovern discussed his proposal for curtailing drug traffic, his policies toward street crime, his ideas about gun control, his feelings about the court system, his hopes for prison reform. By traditional journalistic standards, the speech was important news.

But George McGovern's address was not reported on the evening newscasts of all three national television networks. Although the speech was delivered at noon, giving ABC, CBS, and NBC ample time to prepare news reports, two networks completely ignored the address. Instead, they covered a McGovern motorcade held in Boston later that same day. These reports talked about the size of the crowd and the standing of the South Dakota Senator in the opinion polls, with the camera following the winding motorcade and panning the wildly cheering crowd, as evidenced in this report carried by one network that day:

VIDEO	AUDIO
Anchorman	ANCHORMAN: Democratic presidential candidate George McGovern continued his stepped-up campaign against President Nixon today. In New York, McGovern told a questioner that the Nixon Administration is, in his words, "the most reckless, wasteful, and irresponsible Administration in the history of the country." Here is a political report on McGovern in Boston where he drew one of the biggest crowds of his career.
Reporter with large, wildly cheering crowd in background and motorcade winding slowly through street	REPORTER: It was the sort of crowd every candidate has fantasies about. Even before the motorcade reached Post Office Square, people were spilling into the street, crowding around McGovern's car, ten and twelve deep. In the Square itself there were thousands, so many that any crowd estimate is

VIDEO	AUDIO
Large crowd in square	only a guess. A veteran Boston reporter said it was larger than Lyndon Johnson's in '64, larger than Hubert Humphrey's in '68, the largest in fact since John Kennedy in 1960.
McGovern on speaker's stand	GEORGE MCGOVERN: The first order of business will be to halt the bombing and then terminate our involvement in this tragic war. When I become President of the United States and hold up my hand saying that I swear allegiance to the Constitution of this country, I mean every word of that, with every fiber in my being.
Reporter with crowd as background	REPORTER: The polls all show George McGovern running far behind but time and time again, he will go into a city and see a large crowd like this one, perhaps not this large, but large nevertheless. So it is perhaps understandable that he is mystified by the polls.[1]

On this campaign day, as many campaign days, there were plenty of good pictures but very little hard information. Dramatic film and not substance often governs the content of presidential campaign coverage.

A presidential campaign is particularly well suited to the networks' well-documented preference for good pictures. The campaign is a freewheeling affair, serious, yet carnival-like, offering the networks wide choice in what they can report and what they can ignore. Once in a while, a candidate will make a startling blunder or score a major triumph. Such a banner story must be broadcast, even if network camera crews can capture no exciting pictures. But these events are rare occurrences. On most days, reporters and producers have free rein in their coverage. The typical campaign day will find the candidates making public appearances throughout the country, speaking earnestly about the nation's problems, while immersed in the surrealistic surroundings of frantic motorcades and boisterous rallies. Since nothing earthshaking happens, story possibilities on such a day are almost endless. Network cameras are not forced to focus on the candidate's speeches. The cameras can just as easily be pointed at the motorcades and crowds, the hecklers and the loyalists—that offer action, adventure, people in motion.

What the Networks Fail to Cover—the Candidates' Qualifications to be President

Since television provides the viewer with an almost firsthand look at political candidates, network news should

TABLE 1. HOW THE NETWORKS PRESENTED THE CANDIDATES TO THE VIEWERS (1972 ELECTION)

	ABC	CBS	NBC
Candidate by himself	9%	6%	7%
Candidate with a small number of people	12	13	12
Candidate addressing a meeting or convention	19	23	23
Candidate appearing before a large crowd	60	58	58
	100%	100%	100%

Table percentages are based on all network evening news stories between September 18 and November 6, 1972, which showed the candidates on camera during campaign appearances.

be a powerful medium for informing the electorate about the character and leadership traits of presidential aspirants. Yet, it is not.

Instead of analyzing characters and examing backgrounds, the networks simply parade faces. ABC, CBS, and NBC offer few penetrating reports on the candidates and their personal qualifications for President. They seldom discuss the candidates' personal fitness for office—their moral codes, personal habits and private behaviors, personal reactions to past political stresses, or leadership styles. Likewise the networks avoid intimate interviews that would provide viewers themselves with a chance to study closely presidential candidates. Instead, television news emphasizes superficial pictures of the candidates in action (Table 1). About sixty percent of the time that a presidential candidate was shown on camera during the 1972 general election, he was pictured in a crowd scene. Less than ten percent of the time was the candidate alone, except for a reporter. In the visual world of network news, the candidate naked before the camera is no match for the candidate surrounded by a chanting, jostling mob.

The unrevealing nature of much of the network coverage of presidential candidates is illustrated quite well by this network report about George McGovern:

VIDEO	AUDIO
Anchorman	ANCHORMAN: With Tricia Nixon Cox and Governor Rockefeller on the reviewing stand and Transportation Secretary Volpe as Parade Marshall, the Republicans had apparently preempted New York's Columbus Day celebration, apparently that is until they found Senator McGovern in the line of march.

VIDEO	AUDIO
George McGovern walking in parade	REPORTER: (parade music) George McGovern wooed Italian-Americans by walking twenty-five blocks up Fifth Avenue in the Columbus Day Parade. Some marchers grumbled that politicians ought to go find their own fun and leave other people's parades alone, but McGovern got a generally good reception, stopping at St. Patrick's Cathedral for a few words with Terence Cardinal Cooke. Then McGovern headed for the reviewing stand. He's been complaining all fall that the President keeps using surrogate candidates — stand-ins — instead of campaigning himself and there at the stand was a whole covey of surrogates: Mrs. Cox, Governor Rockefeller, Parade Marshall Volpe, along with Mayor John Lindsay. McGovern stood twenty or thirty feet away. Lindsay, just as in real life, finally left the Republicans and went over to join McGovern, almost hiding his state campaign chairman, former Mayor Robert Wagner. Mrs. Cox smiled a lot and said it was a nice parade. Volpe huffed and puffed about the political impropriety of turning up at parades without an invitation. McGovern said he had been invited by the Ladies Garment Workers Union. Mrs. Cox said she had been to the parade before. The crowd shouted. The surrogates gave interviews. Mrs. Cox smiled some more and the bands kept marching by.[2]
McGovern at Cathedral with Cooke	
McGovern at reviewing stand	
Mrs. Cox, Rockefeller, Volpe together on reviewing stand with Lindsay	
Lindsay joining McGovern	
Mrs. Cox smiling	
Volpe close-up	
McGovern close-up	
Mrs. Cox close-up	
People on reviewing stand Bands marching past	

   The Columbus Day parade story was perfect for television. Good pictures full of sound and fury. Conflict. Personalities. It was quintessential network political coverage. Showing the candidate engulfed in a crowd or stepping off an airplane is precisely the "inside, close-up" view of the candidates that network television touts as so revealing and informative.

About the only time that the candidates' qualifications for President are aired on the evening newscasts comes when one candidate charges that his opponent lacks the talent and strength of purpose to be President. Typical of this treatment in 1972 were McGovern's charges that Nixon was corrupt, and the claims of Nixon confederates that McGovern was inept. Television's journalists, however, certainly made no independent contribution to assessing candidate character in the autumn of 1972.

A detailed content analysis of network evening news during the 1972 general election reveals the limits of television's coverage of presidential candidates. From September 18 to November 6, 1972, the evening newscasts of ABC, CBS, and NBC were examined for any reference to Nixon's or McGovern's qualifications in twelve important personal and leadership areas: their political experience, the foresight of their political actions, their understanding of average citizens, the clarity of their political intentions, their compassion for the less fortunate, their personal trustworthiness, their personal appeal, their susceptibility to political expediency, their ability to remain in control in various situations, their ability to create confidence in their leadership, their tendency toward extremism in their political proposals, and the strength of their political convictions. Any network news reference to either candidate in these twelve areas was recorded, including the number of news seconds given to the reference. Regardless of the source, all references were counted—whether they were contained in the anchorman's lead, the correspondent's narrative, a candidate's remarks, or any other format.

Although all references were included, no matter how fleeting or who made them, it is apparent that network news had no time for candidate analysis during the 1972 general election (Table 2). The ABC evening news spent less than twenty minutes on the candidates' personal and leadership qualifications. The CBS evening news carried only sixteen minutes. And the NBC evening news contributed just eight minutes. As a network average, these minutes represent only one percent of available news time during this period of the presidential election, a time when the campaign was receiving its most intense, continuous coverage. By any

TABLE 2. NETWORK COVERAGE OF 12 LEADERSHIP/ PERSONAL QUALIFICATIONS OF RICHARD NIXON AND GEORGE McGOVERN (SEPTEMBER 18–NOVEMBER 6, 1972)[3]

	ABC Evening News	CBS Evening News	NBC Evening News
Network coverage of Nixon's qualifications:			
Total news minutes for all 12 Nixon qualifications	13:53	9:23	5:02
Average news minutes for each Nixon qualification	1:10	0:47	0:25
Network coverage of McGovern's qualifications:			
Total news minutes for all 12 McGovern qualifications	5:37	7:01	3:03
Average news minutes for each McGovern qualification	0:28	0:35	0:15

NOTE: Data include every explicit reference, regardless of source, to the candidates' qualifications in twelve areas in all network news stories directly about the campaign from September 18–November 6, 1972. A full explanation of procedures is in Appendix C.

standard, the candidates' qualification for office was not a major theme of the evening newscasts.

While it might be said that networks had little obligation to examine Richard Nixon's personal and leadership qualities, since he was the incumbent and had been subject to public scrutiny for more than twenty years, the same argument cannot be made in George McGovern's case. In the fishbowl of presidential politics, McGovern was a neophyte. The public had little information about him. Most voters possessed, at best, only fragmentary knowledge about his personal and leadership characteristics. Yet, ABC, CBS, and NBC devoted almost no time to news reports that would reveal what McGovern was like. During the last two months of the 1972 campaign, the networks on the average gave McGovern's personal and leadership qualities only about five minutes of news time. Virtually nothing was said about his abilities to deal with people or about the kind of leadership he offered. About thirty seconds, as a network average, were spent on each of the twelve personal and leadership qualities as they applied to McGovern. And most of these news seconds came from the lips of his friends and enemies who either extolled his virtues or enumerated his faults. Network anchormen and correspondents paid no attention to describing the kind of man and potential leader George McGovern was.

Some observers would contend that television news has no need to examine the character and values of presidential candidates, that the viewers themselves can make all the necessary meaningful judgments about candidates simply from watching politicians perform in the campaign situations that television provides.[4] Advocates of this thesis would argue that the actions, expressions, mannerisms, and style of the candidate on television reveal his true inner person and character to the steady viewer. If true, surface coverage of presidential aspirants on network news could be justified. But the most serious research on this question would argue against this thesis. As Kurt Lang and Gladys Engel Lang have stated, on the basis of several careful case studies of political events, the conclusions that people draw about electronic political figures are superficial and highly contextual.[5] Strolling down the streets of New York in a Columbus Day parade, haranguing a crowd in a high school gym, or waving at partisans in a motorcade hardly forms the most thought-provoking context in which to assess the personal character of a man who could occupy the White House.

What the Networks Fail to Cover—Candidates on the Issues

Hard issue information is the second victim of television journalism's preference for pictures. A candidate standing before the camera discussing an important campaign issue, such as unemployment, often cannot compete with Charles Kuralt covering a logrolling contest in Idaho or Jack Perkins covering the flag-waving, placard-bobbing, ear-deafening rowdyism of an election rally. Issue stories usually require the networks to present the "talking heads" of the candidates. And, by network standards, those stories are dull.[6]

The networks downplay election issues. Many of the candidates' major issue statements are ignored entirely. When issues are not ignored altogether, they are still rarely the sole topic of the story. Most often, when the networks report anything about issues, the news story is suffused with enough hoopla to make it visually exciting. The result is issue coverage so fleeting and so superficial that it is almost meaningless. A typical illustration of the lip service paid to election issues is this network report on the Nixon campaign:

VIDEO   AUDIO

Anchorman   ANCHORMAN: President Nixon made one of his infrequent campaign trips today, this

VIDEO	AUDIO
	time going through traditionally Republican communities in the New York area promising to do all he can to block what he called "a Congressional spending spree."
Motorcade moving through crowded streets Crowd cheering President McGovern supporters and protestors picketing Nixon's appearance Motorcade winding its way through countryside Motorcade moving through business district People racing in and out of moving buses The Nixons shaking hands with crowd	REPORTER: The Nixon campaign rolled through the wealthy northern suburbs of New York City, attacking Congress, which of course was not there, and warmly embracing the crowds which were on hand. In a written statement issued on arrival in Westchester County, the Republican candidate contended "the time has come to stand up to the big spenders in Congress." He promised to use every weapon to hold down federal spending. The economy, though, wasn't as much a focus of protest as the bombing and Vietnam war, especially among small pockets of pro-McGovern supporters along the way. The fifty-mile motorcade route wound through eleven small cities in the solid Republican county which Nixon carried by 28,000 votes in 1968. With the Veterans Day holiday, schools out, and the route directed through the heart of business districts, the crowds were standing deep at the curbs and, at times, raced dangerously in and out among five photo trucks and seven press buses packed with newsmen trying to observe the action of the most extended day of Nixon campaigning thus far. At a couple of points the President's limousine stopped, and as he worked one side of the crowd, Mrs. Nixon worked the other.[7]

Network neglect of issues is clearly evident from a careful content analysis of the nightly news during the 1972 general election. From September 18 to November 6, 1972, every television news reference to twenty-six different candidates' issue stands was tabulated. The twenty-six issues included all critical issues of the election: Nixon's policies toward China, Russia, inflation, and government spending, and both candidates' policies on the level of military spending, jobs for the jobless, clean government, welfare chiselers, drug trafficking, tax burden, immediate withdrawal from Vietnam, commitments to foreign allies, busing, crime, and amnesty for draft evaders. Each network news reference, and the length of that reference, to any of the twenty-six issue positions was noted, regardless of the source making the reference.

The evening newscasts of ABC had 35 minutes of news time pertaining to these twenty-six candidate issue positions, or only about 80 seconds for each issue during the entire last seven weeks of the 1972 campaign (Table 3). The CBS evening news had 46 minutes in total, or about 105 seconds for each issue. And the nightly news of NBC carried only 26 minutes in total, or about 60 seconds for each of the issue positions. As a network average, only three percent of available news minutes during the 1972 general election were given to these election issues. With the exception of Nixon's Vietnam policy, which accounted for thirty percent of all network time given to the twenty-six issues, the coverage given any single candidate issue position was so minimal, averaging less than 60 seconds, it was meaningless.

Network coverage of George McGovern's policies shows most clearly the neglect of election issues. Although McGovern was on the campaign trail almost every day, discussing a wide range of issues, his policy positions went almost entirely unreported. For instance, although his economic proposals were a cornerstone of his campaign, his stands on joblessness, inflation, welfare, taxation, and government spending received almost no news coverage. His positions on each of these issues averaged less than a minute on the weeknight newscasts of each of the networks. And this includes all the newscasts during the entire last seven weeks of the campaign.

TABLE 3. NETWORK COVERAGE OF THE PLATFORMS/ POLICIES OF RICHARD NIXON AND GEORGE McGOVERN (SEPTEMBER 18–NOVEMBER 6, 1972)

	ABC Evening News	CBS Evening News	NBC Evening News
Network coverage of 15 Nixon policy positions:			
Total news minutes for all 15 Nixon policy positions	29:43	33:42	20:33
Average news minutes for each Nixon policy position	1:59	2:15	1:22
Network coverage of 11 McGovern policy positions:			
Total news minutes for all 11 McGovern policy positions	5:35	12:38	5:41
Average news minutes for each McGovern policy position	0:30	1:09	0:31

NOTE: Data include every explicit reference, regardless of source, to the candidates' positions on twenty-six issues in all network news stories directly about the campaign from September 18–November 6, 1972. A full explanation of procedures is in Appendix C.

Even McGovern's stand on his key issue—withdrawal from Vietnam—received only minimal attention from the networks.

Richard Nixon's policies went equally unreported. Although Nixon did little campaigning, Vice-President Agnew and other Nixon surrogates were on the trail almost daily, and the three networks covered them. But the networks paid little attention to what they were saying about the issues. Every time Spiro Agnew encountered a heckler, the news reported it. Rarely were his statements about Nixon policies given the same attention.

Only the Vietnam peace talks prevented the networks from ignoring major election issues almost entirely. Until rumors of an imminent Vietnam settlement began flowing from the Paris talks about six weeks before Election Day, the networks' routine campaign coverage had no time for issues. The obvious importance of the peace negotiations, however, forced the networks into assessing its effect on the election and airing McGovern's charges and White House denials that the peace efforts were an election ploy. But, had it not been for this coverage in a single policy area, only two percent of available news time, as a network average, would have been given to the candidates' major issue stands.

No explanation readily accounts for network dismissal of issues except that they lack film value. It is not that issues were unimportant in 1972. In fact, the candidates offered the American people one of the clearest policy choices of this century. And although the election's outcome was never in doubt, the campaign had meaning precisely because the candidates did have distinct policy differences. Yet that meaning and those differences went unreported on network news.

What the Networks Do Cover—The Contest:
    Horse Race and Hoopla

One dimension of the election fits perfectly the networks' demand for good pictures. It is the "horse race" aspect of the run for the White House. For a presidential election is surely a super contest with all the elements that are associated with spectacular sports events: huge crowds, rabid followers, dramatic do-or-die battles, winners and losers. It is this part of the election that the networks emphasize (Table 4). During the 1972 general election, as a network average, about nine times as many minutes were given to campaign activity as to the analysis of the candidates' qualifications on key personal and leadership traits and almost four times as many minutes as were given to the candidates' positions on the election's critical issues.

TABLE 4. HOW THE NETWORKS DISTRIBUTED THEIR NEWS MINUTES (1972 ELECTION)[8]

	ABC	CBS	NBC
Time given to campaign activity (e.g., rallies, motorcades, polls, strategies, big labor)	140:58	121:34	130:20
Time given to the candidates' key personal and leadership qualifications for office	19:30	16:24	8:05
Time given to the candidates' stands on key issues of the election	35:19	46:20	26:14

In its own way, a presidential election has all the pageantry, color, glamour, and decisiveness of the Kentucky Derby. Indeed, network reporting treats a presidential election exactly like a horse race. The camera follows the entries around the country trying to capture the drama, excitement, and adventure of a grueling run for the November finish line. The opinion polls are cited frequently, indicating the candidates' positions on the track. The strengths and weaknesses of all the participants are constantly probed, providing an explanation for their position and creating drama about how the race might change as they head down the homestretch. The feverish activity that accompanies the campaign provides the back-barn setting that lends color and "inside-dope" to the coverage. Crowds are essential. Those political activists who fill the auditoriums and city squares, who line the streets and show up at airports, are an indispensable ingredient for the campaign-as-contest theme. The crowd is the rooting section for the candidates, the die-hard railbirds who cheer their entry on, testimony to the drawing power of the candidates and certain proof of what is at stake as they near the finish line.

There can be no doubt that this is the theme, the essence, of television election coverage. The following stories, representing one network's candidate coverage during the final five weekdays of the 1972 campaign, indicate better than any statistics how television news handles a presidential election. (This network's campaign stories for the other weekdays in the final month of the 1972 election are contained in Appendix F):[9]

Tuesday, October 31

The latest Harris Poll shows Nixon has slightly increased his lead over McGovern to 28 percent. (0:29)

McGovern appears to be doing well with the young as reflected in his crowds, but the polls indicate that overall he is not doing that well. McGovern's people believe the polls are wrong and he can win. (0:87)

Pennsylvania is an important state to McGovern. The eastern part of the state is Nixon country. Appalachian Pennsylvania usually supports the Democrats, particularly in the cities. McGovern may be seriously hurt by withholding of union support in Pittsburgh and low registration of black voters. Both candidates have campaigned frequently here, but it looks like McGovern will need a lot more helps if he is to carry the state. (2:05)

Nixon to go on television for first paid political speech of his campaign. He will start to pick up the pace of his campaign in this last week. (0:25)

Wednesday, November 1

Nixon in a radio address said he is doing more for the cities than Johnson did. McGovern said the Democratic Congress deserves the credit. (0:27)

McGovern had a noontime parade through New York City. He was out to attract the ethnic vote and gave a rally in the garment district. A huge crowd assembled to hear McGovern attack Nixon's handling of the economy and Ted Kennedy saying he thought McGovern would come from behind. McGovern canceled a speech in Minnesota because of a sore throat but flew to Chicago to speak tonight. (2:00)

Shriver campaigned in Portland and Seattle today. (0:07)

Agnew ran into a group of hecklers in San Diego. Agnew told demonstrators that since they use fascist tactics they ought to wear brown shirts. Agnew went on to say McGovernism will become an obscure footnote in history. (1:59)

Analysis of Democratic California shows that many Democrats will jump to Nixon. McGovern canvassing is trying to reverse polls that have Nixon leading in the state. Nixon people are working just to get their voters to the polls. (2:17)

Commentary on how Nixon has hardly campaigned and still is far ahead in the polls while McGovern has campaigned frantically. It appears that the electorate cares very little about this election. (0:74)

Thursday, November 2

Mrs. Nixon was heckled in Boston today, and Agnew was heckled yesterday in San Diego. The Nixon people blame McGovern people and the McGovern people said it was a "put-up job" by the GOP. (0:27)

McGovern attended huge rally at the University of Cincinnati. McGovern was heckled by a group of Nixon supporters. McGovern charged that the Agnew hecklers in San Diego had been planted to disrupt McGovern's campaign efforts. Despite the likelihood of Cincinnati going Republican, McGovern's staff people think they have a shot at carrying Ohio. (1:55)

Klein (Nixon's Communication Director) said he thought Nixon would carry at least 45 of the 50 states in the election. (0:17)

McGovern must carry Michigan if he is to have any chance to win. The only important issue to Michigan voters is busing. Wallace's success in the Democratic Party primary illustrates the fact. Most Michigan voters feel Nixon will do what he can to stop busing while McGovern would not. Michigan seems in the Nixon column. (2:20)

Gallup Poll showed that one big area where McGovern lacks support is among blue-collar workers. He is receiving less support among this segment of the public than any Democrat since 1936. (0:26)

In a traditionally Democratic section of Cleveland, workers claimed they would vote for Nixon by a large margin. Over the last six weeks Nixon's support has slightly eroded but still heavily Nixon. (3:47)

Commentary on how ugly recent history must be considered in analyzing why America votes as it does. Search for order and calmness might explain 1972 election results. (2:25)

Friday, November 3

McGovern speaking in Michigan said he is skeptical that peace will come soon. He then went to tape a televised talk for tonight. He is to say that Nixon is deceiving the people. (1:56)

Nixon made his only campaign appearance in Illinois. He fully expects to win Illinois this year. He ignored hecklers and said he wanted peace with honor. He then went to Oklahoma and Rhode Island to help local Republicans. (1:59)

Illinois is an important state for a candidate. Chicago is heavily Democratic and its suburbs are Republican. Southern Illinois is largely Republican with pockets of Democratic strength. As a result, Illinois is fairly evenly divided. Nixon has a lead, but McGovern appears to be on the move according to polls. (2:18)

In Wyoming, Agnew attended an overwhelmingly favorable rally, but his speech was disrupted by a small group of protestors. He accused McGovern of unprecedented meddling in foreign policy. In Denver, Agnew was again heckled. (2:13)

Shriver attacked Nixon's delay in signing the Paris agreement. He said voters might be swayed if they believe Nixon is letting Thieu block peace efforts. (2:17)

From April 8 to October 26 McGovern committees spent $18 million. During this same period, Nixon committees spent twice as much. Nixon people spent even more when those funds not reported are included. Campaign spending is skyrocketing. (0:57)

Monday, November 6

McGovern's last day of campaigning took him from New York City to California and then to South Dakota by the end of the day. He said Nixon has deceived the people on peace. He campaigned to huge crowds in Philadephia at noon. McGovern reflected on campaign and said he would not run again in 1976 if he lost. (1:51)

Nixon's only campaign act on this last campaign day was to tape a televised statement. Nixon's campaign appearances have been very minimal and he seems confident of victory. (1:31)

Shriver's strategy for the last day of the campaign was to appear in as many places as possible. He visited five key states in the day. He started in Pittsburgh and then held a press conference in Cleveland. (1:45)

Agnew appeared super-confident in Philadelphia. Protestors were restrained. He spoke at the Fraternal Order of Police. He then went to Virginia to campaign for a senatorial candidate. (1:51)

Commentary on tremendous amount of money thrown into campaign and how most money still comes from big contributors. (1:53)

The polls show the likelihood of a Nixon landslide. The Gallup Poll showed McGovern trailing by 26 percent. This is the second biggest lead any incumbent has had since the polls began. (0:35)

Commentary that the 1972 election will probably be remembered as the campaign in which the President campaigned so little. It seems analogous to the 1944 Roosevelt campaign in which FDR hardly campaigned. It seems the voters suffered from the lack of the campaign. (0:61)

Quite clearly, this network's campaign coverage focused on the election as a horse race. The 1972 election itself demanded no such coverage; it was never much of a contest at all. But on network television, the contest theme was carried to the campaign's very end, at the expense of the election's issues and the candidates' qualifications for office.

Chapter 2
Network Evening News and an Informed Electorate

It must be recognized that television has necessarily become the medium through which the great majority of voters get their news.[1]

—*Richard M. Nixon*

By appearing on a television news program, the candidate is guaranteed an audience that has some interest in public affairs . . . For this audience largely dependent [on television news] for its information about current events, news programs form the windows to their minds.[2]

—*Robert MacNeil, author and television correspondent*

FROM the birth of the republic and the concomitant rise of the local partisan press, the mass media have borne the responsibility for keeping Americans informed about public affairs. To be sure, the media have other obligations—to watch-dog government officials, to cater to public tastes, and even to make a profit. But above all else, the acknowledged role of the media in American democracy is to serve the public's need to know about government actions. This responsibility heightens during a presidential election, when an ordinarily uninterested citizenry seems more willing to listen and learn about politics. Edwin Diamond, mass communication critic and scholar, has stated clearly this conception of the role of a democratic press: "The media's chief job in a campaign is not to elect, or defeat, but to make sure that sufficient information, in understandable form, is available to the voters who do the electing."[3]

In today's world, the three major television networks carry a large share of this responsibility. Each year more Americans depend on network newscasts for their campaign information. In turn, presidential candidates rely increasingly on television news to carry their messages to the electorate. As a result, the networks have become the preeminent medium for the conduct and surveillance of presidential elections.

Audience data for network news dramatically illustrates just how preeminent the medium has become. Each weekday evening during a presidential campaign, the networks broadcast news of the election to a national audience that includes about one in every six Americans. According to the A. C. Nielsen Company, which measures television audiences, a typical weekday evening will find almost ten million viewers turned to the ABC evening news with Harry Reasoner, more than fifteen million viewers watching the CBS evening news with Walter Cronkite, and almost fifteen million viewers seeing the NBC evening news with John Chancellor. These television news audiences are far larger and more regionally diverse than the readership of any American newspaper. Indeed, no one has ever spoken to America's voters as directly and as regularly as the anchormen of the networks' evening newscasts.

The need of this vast audience for basic political information, then, is obvious. And if the networks are fulfilling their responsibility, regular viewers of nightly newscasts ought to show increased political knowledge during a presidential election. Unfortunately they do not. A systematic study of network news effects reveals viewers learn little relevant knowledge from watching television news. Quite bluntly,

ABC, CBS, and NBC are failing to live up to the media's traditional responsibility to keep the public politically informed.

The Networks' Impact on Voters' Issue Awareness

Of all the information voters obtain through the mass media during a presidential campaign, knowledge about where the candidates stand on the issues is among the most vital. If people are to vote intelligently, they must be aware of the policy positions of the candidates. If voters know such information, they have a chance of casting their ballots wisely.

Television does not help the electorate to vote on the issues. Based on interviews conducted with potential voters during the 1972 general election, this conclusion is simply inescapable. At the beginning of the general election, and again at the end, the *same* people were asked where they thought the candidates stood on a wide range of election issues. Virtually every important 1972 election issue was included among those about which these people were questioned—Nixon's policies toward Vietnam, China, Russia, taxes, government spending, commitments to foreign allies, military spending, amnesty, unemployment, crime, drugs, and busing, and McGovern's stands on military spending, Vietnam withdrawal, amnesty, political corruption, taxes, and unemployment. Because the same people were questioned at the start and finish, it is possible to determine how much their issue information improved during the campaign.

Regular viewing of network news had no influence on how much these people learned (Table 1).

On about half the election issues, regular viewers of network news became better informed during the campaign than nonregular viewers. But on the other half, people who did not bother to watch the evening news regularly became more knowledgeable than those who did. And on the typical issue stand, both frequent and infrequent viewers increased their issue awareness almost at the same rate. Regular view-

TABLE 1. THE IMPACT OF NETWORK NEWS EXPOSURE ON PEOPLE'S ISSUE AWARENESS DURING 1972 GENERAL ELECTION

NOTE: Figures represent percent increase or percent decrease (−) in people's issue information during the 1972 general election. A full explanation of figures is contained in Appendix D.

	Nonregular viewers of network news	Regular viewers of network news
	%	%
Nixon policies:		
Vietnam war	4	11
Government spending	14	3
Military spending	27	36
Busing	35	35
China	38	32
Russia	25	28
Foreign commitments	37	50
Taxes on upper incomes	7	0
Law and order	2	− 6
Jobs for the unemployed	15	16
Amnesty	41	49
Drugs	8	7
McGovern policies:		
Military spending	63	58
Vietnam withdrawal	38	67
Amnesty	38	31
Political corruption	− 4	9
Taxes on upper incomes	14	40
Jobs for the unemployed	45	45
Average on all issues	25	28

ers had a 28 percent increase in information. Nonregular viewers had a 25 percent increase. Stated differently, those individuals who faithfully tuned in network news during the election learned not much more than people who spent that time doing something else.

By way of comparison, newspaper readers became much better informed on these same election issues during the 1972 campaign (Table 2). People who took time to read their daily newspaper regularly showed a significantly larger information gain than occasional readers. With the exception of a single issue, regular newspaper readers acquired a greater awareness of where the candidates stood on the issues. On the typical issue, the gain in information for newspaper readers was nearly twice that for the people who seldom looked at the newspaper's political coverage. On foreign policy and domestic policy issues, on Nixon's issue positions and McGovern's issue positions, the newspaper reader came to understand better what the candidates had done or said they would do. Frequent readers had a 35 percent increase in their issue awareness; infrequent readers only an 18 percent increase. No doubt can exist that the minutes people spent reading their newspaper, unlike the minutes they gave to watching network news, clearly increased their issue awareness.

Of course, most people cannot be neatly labeled as newspaper readers or television news viewers. Although some voters depend more heavily on one medium or the other, many voters are equally avid news viewers and newspaper readers and still other voters take no interest in either information source. So an accurate estimate of the impact of network news and the newspaper requires that people's viewing and reading habits be considered simultaneously. When this is done, it becomes even clearer that television news is uninformative and the newspaper is highly educational. In the category of people who were neither regular television news viewers nor regular newspaper readers, there was a 19 percent increase in information during the 1972 election. This

TABLE 2. THE IMPACT OF NEWSPAPER READING ON PEO-
PLE'S ISSUE AWARENESS DURING 1972 GENERAL
ELECTION[4]

NOTE: Figures represent percent increase or percent decrease in people's issue information during the
1972 general election. A full explanation of
figures is contained in Appendix D.

	Nonregular newspaper readers	Regular newspaper readers
	%	%
Nixon policies:		
Vietnam war	− 5	22
Government spending	3	13
Military spending	21	34
Busing	31	43
China	19	51
Russia	12	41
Foreign commitments	22	62
Taxes on upper incomes	9	− 1
Law and order	−12	10
Jobs for the unemployed	8	21
Amnesty	36	57
Drugs	2	12
McGovern policies:		
Military spending	50	67
Vietnam withdrawal	32	66
Amnesty	24	45
Political corruption	− 1	11
Taxes on upper incomes	16	38
Jobs for the unemployed	48	43
Average on all issues	18	35

increase was as much as the gain in issue information among
people who watched television news regularly but who did
not pay much attention to the newspaper. By comparison,

among people who read the newspaper regularly but who
did not bother to watch the evening news regularly there was
a 34 percent increase in issue awareness. In other words, if
people only watched network news, they did not come to
know more than people who ignored the news media during
the fall of 1972. If they only read the newspaper, however,
they learned substantially more.

It might be thought, nevertheless, that television has some
impact on a limited group of voters. Some experts have spec-
ulated that the young, women, the less affluent, and the less
well-educated are highly influenced by television news. The
thinking behind this speculation is that these groups, although traditionally less interested in politics than other
groups, find television's version of the news appealing
enough to pay some attention. If this speculation is correct,
such groups should become more knowledgeable from
watching the evening news.

But during the 1972 general election they did not become
better informed. None of these groups learned much from
watching network news, as their percent increase in knowledge on the average issue makes clear:

	Nonregular Viewers	Regular Viewers
	%	%
Men	26	26
Women	24	29
Less than high school	15	18
High school graduate	23	26
More than high school	33	37
Income under $7,000	18	19
Income of $7,000–$13,999	30	30
Income $14,000 and over	30	36
30 years of age or under	21	18
31–59 years of age	26	30
60 years of age or over	18	25

Neither men nor women, the uneducated nor well educated, the poor nor the wealthy, the young nor the old greatly improved their issue information by tuning in television news. Newspaper reading, by comparison, informed each of these groups of voters:

	Nonregular Readers	Regular Readers
	%	%
Men	19	33
Women	16	37
Less than high school	6	29
High school graduate	16	34
More than high school	27	40
Income under $7,000	15	27
Income of $7,000–$13,999	20	39
Income $14,000 and over	25	39
30 years of age or under	16	41
31–59 years of age	21	36
60 years of age or over	1	35

Every category in the electorate became much better informed if they regularly read a newspaper's political sections.

In summary, then, all the evidence leads to an inescapable conclusion—television news adds little to the average voter's understanding of election issues. Network news may be fascinating. It may be highly entertaining. But it is simply not informative.

Uninformative News

This conclusion conflicts with conventional wisdom. Most politicians, journalists, and scholars contend that television network news has a powerful impact on the thinking of the American voter. One reason is cited repeatedly: Television is the only mass medium that communicates with pictures, thus giving voters a penetrating eyewitness look at the campaign.

It is in the nature of pictures to reflect action. It is very difficult for them to reflect thought or policy.[5]

—*Charles Curran, Director-General, BBC*

Ironically, however, the reliance on pictures is a major reason why network news is an unsuccessful source of election information. The networks' insistence on a videocentric portrayal of the campaign undermines their informational impact on viewers. Not that film is necessarily a poor communicator. At times, film can have a powerful effect. When pictures fully capture a visually dramatic event, as news film did of the attempted assassination of George Wallace during the 1972 primaries, they can have a jolting impact on viewers. But few campaign issues can be told well with pictures.

Equally important is the fact that although a television signal may travel at the speed of light from the speaker to the viewer, information is transferred from speaker to viewer no faster than the speaker talks. And very few words can be uttered in a thirty-minute newscast. More precisely, all the words spoken on a network evening newscast will fit, with room to spare, on the front page of a newspaper.[6] When a large portion of that limited number of words is devoted to campaign hijinks, the networks in effect rule out the coverage of more relevant election information.

People's television viewing habits also significantly affect how and what they learn from network news. Since most people watch passively and are not deeply involved in what they are viewing, television informs slowly, through repetition and familiarity. Take product advertising as an example. Although television viewers see a score of televised ads in an evening's viewing, they do not, upon turning off their sets, immediately race to the nearest store to purchase the ballyhooed products. In fact, people give only passing attention to most televised advertising, and as research has discovered, most viewers cannot remember what an ad was about even a minute or two after it was shown.[7] People are simply not paying close enough attention. Over longer periods of time, however, and after repeated exposures to advertisements, many viewers are not only aware of the products, but may associate jingles or catchwords with them. Gradually, the products advertised on television become part of their awareness.[8]

Audiences learn from television entertainment programs in the same way. Viewers of *Gunsmoke* or *All in the Family* do not watch from the edge of their seats, soaking up everything flashed on the screen. A particularly gripping scene may engross them temporarily, but they are normally uninvolved. Consequently, the impressions gained from any single show are usually faint and fleeting. After repeated viewings, however, the prime-time audience associates specific traits with television characters like Colombo, Archie Bunker, and Rhoda, and acquires information about them and orientations toward them.

The importance of repetition can be illustrated in still another context. Few experts contend that televised violence has an immediate impact on behavior.[9] Cases in which individuals have mimicked gross acts of violence shown on television are few. But over time, television programming gradually may lessen some Americans' abhorrence of violence and make manifest otherwise latent violent tendencies in some smaller, unknown portion of the population.

The viewing of network news is no different than watching televised advertising or prime-time whodunits. Indeed for many viewers, network news, because it contends with dinner hour clamor, may receive even less attention than other programming. In any case, many viewers have only a hazy memory of what they have seen on network news. Among people who claimed to have recently watched network news, only one in three were able to recall accurately a news story they had seen. The other two in three viewers had only a vague recollection of any specific news report or were totally unable to recall any news story at all. Many viewers admitted that they simply did not pay that much attention to the news, even when they tuned it in almost nightly:[10]

> To tell the truth, I don't remember what I saw. I don't watch the news that closely.
> —43-year-old housewife

> Sometimes the news just goes in one ear and out the other. Unless something really impresses me, I don't pay much attention.
> —36-year-old factory worker

> It's so repetitious. Seems like the same thing over and over again, so I don't pay much attention.
> —61-year-old salesman

This habit of uninvolved viewing severely restricts the capacity of network news to communicate because only recurring news themes are likely to penetrate viewer awareness. The single news story may attract the viewer temporarily, but its specific impact normally passes as quickly as the next item appears on the screen. There are, of course, dramatic exceptions, such as the attempted assassination of Wallace, that stick in the mind, are thought about, talked about, recalled at a later time. For the most part, however, only news material that appears again and again becomes part of the viewers' political awareness.

Network coverage of a campaign's issues has none of the virtues that might make it informative.

First, most election issues are mentioned so infrequently that viewers could not possibly learn about them. From September 18 to November 6 of the 1972 campaign, most candidate issues were only mentioned *two* or *fewer* times on network news, amounting to about once every three or four weeks.

Second, most issue references are so fleeting that they could not be expected to leave an impression on viewers. On all three networks during the 1972 election, more than 50 percent of candidate issue mentions took place in news segments of twenty seconds or less, and most of these occurred in time spans of ten seconds or less. It was the unusual isssue reference that lasted a minute or more—only 20 percent of those on ABC, 13 percent of CBS's, and 14 percent of NBC's were of this duration.

Third, the candidates' issue positions generally were reported in ways guaranteed to make them elusive. Often, issue references were only part of the audio while the news film pictured the candidate getting off an airplane, wading through a crowd, or riding in a motorcade. There were some exceptions in 1972. The CBS evening news, for example, did a few lengthy reports on major election issues during the campaign's final days. But not more than ten percent of the time were issues the central focus of network news reports.

The upshot of all this is that television news provides an impossible learning situation. When the typical election issue is mentioned once a month, for less than twenty seconds, in a mix of extraneous news material, the certain consequence is viewer ignorance. ABC, CBS, and NBC may have allowed Americans to "see" the campaign, but in so doing they have added nothing of substance to the voters' civic education.

Chapter 3
Network Evening News and the Images of Candidates

Television gives voters the chance to see presidential candidates close-up, almost to the bone.[1]

—*John F. Kennedy*

The TV candidate, then, is measured . . . against Mike Douglas. How well does he handle himself? Does he mumble, does he twitch, does he make me laugh? Do I feel warm inside? Style becomes substance. The medium is the massage and the masseur gets the votes.[2]

—*Joe McGinniss,* The Selling of the President 1968

We have to be very clear on this point: that the response is to the image, not to the man. . . . It's not what's there that counts, it's what's projected—and carrying it one step further, it's not what the candidate projects but rather what the voter receives. And this impression often depends more on the medium and its use than it does on the candidate himself.[3]

—*Raymond Price, political consultant to Richard Nixon*

IN electronic politics, one theme emerges again and again: Television is a visual medium, and to use it effectively, a candidate must project the proper "image," or picture of himself, to the viewer.[4]

Most certainly, the uniqueness of television as a news source rests on the power of pictures to communicate. Network news executives insist that tapes, film, and graphics are as essential as the reporter's words to telling a television news story. In a presidential campaign, this means giving as much emphasis to what candidates *do* in their day-to-day appearances as to what they *say* in their public statements. The candidate-in-action is the picture network news feels compelled to broadcast.

With TV came the end of bloc voting in politics, a form of specialism and fragmentism that won't work since TV. Instead of the voting bloc, we have the icon, the inclusive image. Instead of a political viewpoint or platform, the inclusive political posture or stance.[5]

—*Marshall McLuhan,* Understanding Media

Accepting Marshall McLuhan's dictum that television is a "cool" medium which better transmits images than issues, media consultants encourage their candidate-clients to exploit this network bias. Operating on the assumption that images, more than either issues or parties, win votes, these high-priced advisers want their candidates to engage in televised image-making. Downplayed are the candidates' words; upgraded is their appearance. According to Joseph Napolitan, a noted campaign adviser who managed Hubert Humphrey's campaign in 1968, "it's not what you say, it's how you say it. The general impression that is left is a lot more important than the individual words and phrases."[6]

The media adviser works hard at image-making. The adviser "exploits the best features of the candidate's personality to form the 'television personality.'"[7] Ideally the candidate will appear to the television audience as "pleasant, not abrasive; have a clear, but not too specific, personality; be self-assured, even cocky, but not pretentious; be articulate, but not erudite or glib; be courageous but also cautious; and appear handsome, but not too pretty."[8] The consultant's overriding concern is with how candidates say what they say, and how they look when they say it. The unabashed purpose is to leave a favorable image with the television audience.

Political image-making on television is reminiscent of a scene from William Sansom's *A Contest of Ladies* in which Mr. Preedy, a vacationing Englishman, makes his first appearance on the beach of a summer hotel in Spain:

> . . . it was time to institute a little parade, the parade of the Ideal Preedy. By devious handling, he gave any who wanted to look a chance to see the title of his book—a Spanish translation of Homer, classic thus, but not daring, cosmopolitan too—and then gathered together his beachwrap and bag into a neat sand-resistant pile (Methodical and Sensible Preedy), rose slowly to stretch at ease his huge frame (Big Cat Preedy) and tossed aside his sandals (Carefree Preedy after all).

> . . . a dive straight into the water, thereafter smoothing into a strong, splashless crawl towards the horizon. But of course not really to the horizon. Quite suddenly he would turn on to his back and thrash great white splashes with his legs, somehow thus showing that he could have swum further had he wanted to. . . . The point was to appear to be so used to the sea, the Mediterranean, and this particular beach, that one might as well be in the sea as out of it.[9]

In their desire to create positive televised images, the candidates accede to, and even encourage, network coverage of campaign hoopla. For it is the candidates, after all, that create the action-settings that trivialize their thoughts and misrepresent political substance. Since television images cannot be created without first gaining access to the airwaves, candidates are eager to please network desires. If television news wants action-pictures, candidates will concoct them at every stop.

The influence on presidential candidates of television's picture requirement should not be underestimated. Almost all campaign rallies and almost everything about them—their timing, setting, and even their function—are geared to create pictures for network news. This behind-the-scenes story, carried by one network during the 1972 campaign, reveals how well planned these appearances are:

VIDEO	AUDIO
Band playing in background as reporter talks Motorcade moving through Atlanta Crowd lining the streets Bands playing Confetti falling on motorcade	REPORTER: A "Dixie for Nixon" rally is the look the candidate wanted for this Atlanta noon hour, and that's what he got. A textbook demonstration of how successful a campaign motorcade can be when money is unlimited, advance work is expert, and when the candidate brings with him the canopy of the Presidency. A large crowd gave a loud welcome, part of the crowd's size attributed to a last-minute paid radio and newspaper blitz urging people to turn out. High school bands by the dozen were bused in. Blowing machines, pre-positioned high in buildings, pumped out quick-cut confetti. A near perfect setting for campaign talk.
Nixon speaking	NIXON: . . . biggest one we've ever had. It was very warm, very friendly, as Atlanta crowds always are. This kind of thing, of course, is enjoyable—the opportunity to see people and the rest of the country. And I'll do as much as I can between now and the election, but I have to be President first.
Reporter speaking	REPORTER: Today's production was directed from the airport and elsewhere around

AUDIO
town by Harry Dent, former aide to Senator
Strom Thurmond, now a top White House
adviser, and an architect for Mr. Nixon's so-
called "Southern strategy."[10]

Just as the networks delight in reporting such nonevents,
the candidates are eager to create them because they are convinced that their images depend on it. They believe these television appearances relay a message to the viewer. The message is that the candidate's capacity for leadership is mirrored in the crowd's reaction, his character is portrayed in
the close-ups of his face, his abilities can be measured by the
confidence he projects.

The Images of Committed Voters: Seeing What They Want To See

Despite the efforts of presidential candidates to exploit
television's visual dimension, and the willingness of ABC,
CBS, and NBC to film and broadcast these exploits, the images of White House contenders are influenced only margin-
ally by the style and appearance they exhibit in television
news appearances.

Among those people who are committed to a candidate because of party or issues, television fails at image-making because it cannot overcome this commitment. These voters see
what they want to see when the candidates appear on television. "The candidate" looks good. The opposition candidate
looks bad. What is actually televised matters little. This phe-
nomenon is called *selective perception,* and extensive scientific
research, and common experience, indicates its power.[11]

Among the more interesting experiments on human subjects are those testing perceptions through a binocularlike
device called a multiscope. In one such experiment, a re-
searcher placed the image of the Christian cross on one of
the far lenses of a multiscope and an image of the Star of

David on the other far lens. Then, he had a group of people, comprised half of Jews and half of Christians, look into the multiscope and indicate what they saw. The Jews unfailingly said they saw the Star of David and the Christians indicated seeing the cross. Although their eyes were transmitting both images to their minds, the image consistent with their predispositions dominated. Indeed, it was the only one they saw.[12]

Most people have a biased view of what they see, distorted by their creed, race, class, politics, and a host of other experiences and outlooks. They view the world through tinted glasses, their perceptions distorted by their perspectives and prejudices. Whites and blacks can watch the same confrontation between a policeman and a black and emerge with widely divergent views of what occurred. Working men and businessmen can be embroiled in a labor dispute, listen to the same arguments, see the same activity, and yet disagree violently on what occurred. It is not that one side is wrong and the other is right. It is more that each side is bringing different viewpoints to the situation, viewpoints that structure so decisively what they see that each side might just as well be seeing different things.

Black and White

A study conducted by Allport and Postman indicates the potentially distorting role of personal bias. In their experiment, they showed subjects a picture of a fight taking place on a subway train. One of the quarreling men in the picture was Negro, the other was white. The *white* man held the knife in his hand. Other subway passengers were looking on.

Each subject who saw the picture was instructed to describe it in great detail to a second subject who could not see the picture. The second subject was then told to relay what he had heard to a third subject, and so on.

By the time the story was relayed to the last subject, it had often changed considerably. One of the major changes that happened with some frequency was that the knife which had been in the white man's hand, was said to be in the *black* man's hand.[13]

Most Americans have political biases. Most are loyalists in one way or another, whether their loyalty involves partisanship, group factions, or preferred public policies.[14] Not being political eunuchs, they see candidates through their political desires. The candidate who shares their biases gains stature. His image improves. The candidate who opposes the biases loses stature, and his image deteriorates.

Any person who has been in a room filled with die-hard Republicans and Democrats, watching television while a President justifies his actions on a controversial partisan policy, knows firsthand the impact of selective perception. One group sees sincerity and concern in every gesture, expression, and inflection. The other sees manipulation, crass politics, insincerity. They are watching the same President make the same movements and say the same things, but they might as well be viewing a different person.

Candidates for the presidency elicit the same reaction. Short, noisy, and intense, presidential campaigns bring a great change in the political climate. Politics shifts into high gear; propaganda fills the airwaves; people are asked to pick a side, to stand with one candidate against the other. Yet it is well known that perceptual defenses are at their highest when people are subject to obvious efforts at persuasion. Quite simply, because voters have their guards up, a presidential campaign is an unlikely environment for manipulation to flourish.[15]

Viewers' reactions to campaign story after campaign story reveals the strong pull of bias on what they see. During the 1972 election, for example, George McGovern held a continuing series of rallies, and most evenings, ABC, CBS, and NBC news carried short excerpts from these sagas. In staging these rallies, the McGovern strategy was clear: surrounded by large, friendly crowds, he sought to convey the image of a capable leader, morally righteous, whose growing appeal was mirrored in the thousands turning out for his rallies. Not everyone got the message. For those people whose politics were in tune with McGovern, his televised image was indeed a positive one:[16]

The people [at the rally] were really behind him.
—66-year-old retired postal worker

He looks so able. I think he's very able.
—42-year-old housewife

He is so friendly and sincere. He will make a good President.
—51-year-old teacher

He's a good, honest man. You can see that.
—25-year-old secretary

But to people whose politics were opposed to McGovern, his evening news appearances projected a quite different image:

Just the sight of him burns me up.
—41-year-old laborer

He is boring.
—31-year-old housewife

I don't like him. I wasn't impressed.
—52-year-old housewife

Can't believe what you see. It would be worse with him.
—65-year-old small businessman

He's a weak sister. You can see that immediately.
—27-year-old worker

Different people were watching the same George McGovern on the screen, but clearly, they were not seeing the same man. The fact is, McGovern's news appearances were not creating a televised image, but providing voters an opportunity to express their own political views. Their response was not to the image, but to the politics George McGovern personified.

More systematic evidence on the inability of television news appearances to alter people's images comes from the *pattern of change* in people's images during the 1972 general election campaign. At the start and end of the campaign, the *same* people were asked to judge both Nixon and McGovern on seven image dimensions. Because the same individuals were questioned each time, an accurate estimate is possible of how their images of the two candidates changed during the campaign.

Their image changes leave little doubt that television news image-making had no influence on committed voters (See Table 3 in Appendix E). Among voters favoring Nixon, Nixon's image had a 35 percent improvement and McGovern's image had a 25 percent decline. This was true both for people who were regular viewers of the evening news and those who were not. On the other hand, people who preferred McGovern had the exact opposite changes in their images. McGovern's image underwent a 20 percent improvement and Nixon's image suffered a 20 percent decline. Here again, this happened both for frequent and infrequent viewers of network newscasts.

Thus, even if people watched television news frequently and thus had plenty of opportunity to observe the candidates' so-called "televised images," what they saw played no part in their impressions of the candidates.

People who know what they want from politics, then, respond to the candidates in terms of politics, not television. Cast in a role that is overtly political and partisan, unavoidable during the heat of a presidential campaign, the candidates are seen in political and partisan terms. To assume that a presidential candidate appearing on the Johnny Carson show is somehow evaluated as a television performer, as comedians, singers, and actors are, borders on the absurd. To further assume that a presidential candidate appearing in network news stories, surrounded by cheering partisans, sharing the speaker's platform with political dignitaries, talking about political matters, and acting out a political scenario is viewed for his television personality and not his politics, is even more absurd.

The Images of Undecided Voters: Nothing to See

Perhaps televised image-making works only on the undecided voter. These people often have no strong feelings about politics and, usually, lack even the most elementary knowledge of the candidates.[17] If any group of voters would seem easy prey for televised image-making, it is this group of Americans.

But even the candidate evaluations of undecided voters cannot be manipulated by the image efforts of presidential contenders. Just like committed voters, the candidate images of undecided voters adjust to their candidate preference, not their television news exposure. The data on 1972 undecided voters, people who sometime during the general election were uncertain about backing Nixon or McGovern, confirm the point. Until they made up their mind which candidate to support, their images of Nixon and McGovern changed very little and in no consistent direction, regardless of their exposure to the candidates' televised images. *After* they had selected their candidate, however, their images changed substantially and in an obvious direction. For those selecting Nixon, his image showed a 35 percent improvement and McGovern's image suffered a 25 percent decline among both regular and non-regular news viewers. For those who chose McGovern, his image underwent a 40 percent improvement and Nixon's image had a 50 percent decline among both those who watched the evening news frequently and those who did not.[18]

The most likely explanation why presidential candidates' image efforts on television news have no influence on undecided voters is because such appearances really contain nothing to see. Empty posturing before the television camera means nothing to the uncommitted voter because it says nothing important about the candidate's ability to lead the nation. Just what impression are people supposed to get from seeing a presidential aspirant strut like the NBC peacock?

Undecided voters may not have a strong commitment to politics, but they are not suckers for contrived postures. They have a healthy suspicion that politicians are out to finagle them, and their suspicions increase during the intense propaganda of a presidential campaign. Superficial image-making on network news certainly will not be the source of their candidate images. Perhaps undecided voters would sit up and take notice if the candidates did something worthy of note. But a candidate prancing on the screen gets no meaningful reaction. The only consequence of that kind of emptiness is that the candidate ends up playing a handmaiden to the network practice of glutting America's television screens with visual nonsense.

Does Television Affect Images Early in the Campaign?

Although television news appearances have no influence on people's images during the *general* election, might not television be important earlier in the campaign? Particularly for a relatively unknown candidate, it might be thought that television news would be critical during the initial formation of that candidate's image.

Although Richard Nixon had been in the public spotlight for many years, and had an image unlikely to be affected much by what happened, early or late, in the 1972 campaign, George McGovern was truly a newcomer. McGovern was probably the least well-known presidential nominee since the advent of television, having come from almost nowhere in public recognition and support to capture the Democratic nomination. McGovern relied heavily on network news to carry his campaign to the American people, and, if television news appearances influence the public's image of presidential candidates, it should have been evident in the viewers' appraisal (for better or worse) of the South Dakota

Senator.[19] Now clearly, McGovern's television image did not influence viewers' judgments during the general election. But did his news appearances affect people's images earlier in the campaign?

Available evidence provides *no* indication that it did. McGovern's public image, when the general election campaign began, was an obvious outgrowth of the politics he advocated, the actions he had taken, and how people felt about his political record and intentions. His televised image played no role.

As the voters came to know him, George McGovern was a politician who, above all, wanted to get the United States out of Vietnam immediately; he also wanted to reorder some of America's priorities, calling for more emphasis on liberal domestic programs, many of which were to aid the disadvantaged. While his early campaign provided dramatic victories for a liberal cause, his later efforts were marred by a series of ill-conceived programs, which McGovern first embraced and then had to repudiate; by his selection of Senator Thomas Eagleton as his running-mate, and then his abandonment of Eagleton for Shriver; by his initial rejection of "old" politics, and then his return to traditional partisan strategies.

These experiences with McGovern, and how they meshed with their own political desires, helped voters shape their image of the Democratic candidate at the beginning of the 1972 campaign (Chart 1). Three things are apparent about McGovern's image in early September of 1972. First, regardless of people's politics, they agreed on McGovern's strong and weak points. His strengths were perceived to be his compassion for the less fortunate, his sincerity, his interest in people's problems, and his search for political answers. People who liked his politics, were ambivalent, or even opposed to his political philosophy reserved their highest marks for his humaneness. But McGovern's series of campaign blunders, misdirections, and reversals undermined confidence in his leadership and revealed that he was not above political expediency. And it was in these areas that people had their lowest regard for George Stanley McGovern.

Chart 1. George McGovern's Image Among People with Different Political Orientations and Different Media Habits (September, 1972)[20]

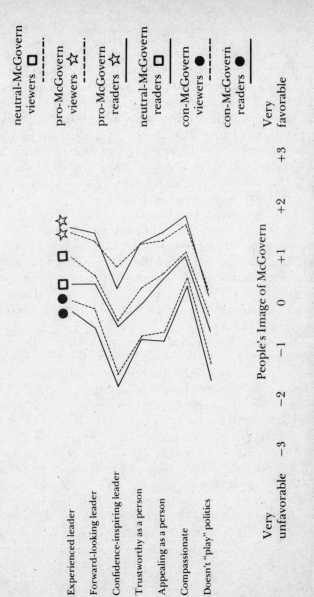

NOTE: People were classified as *pro-McGovern*, *neutral-McGovern*, or *con-McGovern* depending on how close their policy preferences on 11 issues were to the stated policy stands of George McGovern. Further, people were classified as *television viewers* or *newspaper readers* depending on which news medium they relied upon most heavily.

Not everyone, however, had equally favorable and unfavorable judgments of McGovern. A second fact about McGovern's image is that those people who shared his political outlook had clearly more positive images of him than those neutral to his politics who, in turn, had clearly better impressions of him than those opposed to his philosophy. This pattern was true in every instance—whether people were evaluating his experience, his trustworthiness, his foresight, his personal appeal, his compassion, his leadership, or his penchant for playing politics.

The third feature of McGovern's image is that the extent to which voters used the media did not influence their evaluation of him. Those people who relied mainly on television, and those relying mainly on the newspaper, had nearly identical impressions of McGovern. This was as true for their judgments of his personal qualities as it was for their feelings about his leadership qualities. The medium was not the message. It is that simple.

Two other factors totally overwhelm any influence that television may have on candidates' images. First, images depend on what the candidates represent—what party they belong to, what actions they have taken, what policies they advocate. Second, images depend on how the voter feels about what the candidates represent—how the voter feels about the candidates' party, past actions, and future policies. For almost every voter, a candidate's image depends on these two influences, and not on whether he looks good or bad on television. Image-making is best seen as a process where images emerge from a combination of a candidate's actions and voters' political outlooks. The mass media, including television news, play a role in this process; serving to inform the electorate about the candidate. But it is what the candidate does in response to real events and what he stands for on matters of significance that is important, not the medium that communicates this information.

The point can be further underscored by considering the electorate's response to some of the major political figures of the past decade. George C. Wallace is loved and hated, not for his television personality, but because of what he stands for. Despite his ease in using television, John F. Kennedy (before assassination sainted his image) was admired and disliked for his party, his policies, and his religion, and not his television manner. The Lyndon B. Johnson who triumphantly rode to victory in the 1964 election had a badly tarnished image by 1968, ruined not by his television appearance but by a disastrous war in Vietnam. And no doubt Barry Goldwater's views about Social Security and nuclear weapons were the source of his undoing.

The long and short of images is that voters are not fools. Claims that the public's images can be manipulated by shallow television theatrics take the voters for dupes. The American voter judges presidential aspirants by politics, not entertainment. Voters arrive at their image of a candidate by judging where he stands politically and by assessing his significant accomplishments and failures.[21] A smiling presidential candidate, engulfed by thousands of adoring admirers, may make for good television, but it is not the basis on which the electorate evaluates potential leaders. That evaluation is based on politics.

Television's image-making power is a myth.

Chapter 4
Network Evening News and the Public Agenda

The power of the press in America is a primordial one. It sets the agenda of public discussion. . . . It determines what people will talk and think about—an authority that in other nations is reserved for tyrants, priests, parties and mandarins.[1]
—*Theodore White*, The Making of the President 1972

The press is significantly more than a purveyor of information and opinion. It may not be successful much of the time in telling people what to think, but it is stunningly successful in telling its readers what to think about.[2]
—*Bernard Cohen*, The Press, the Public and Foreign Policy

INCREASINGLY, the argument is heard that the mass media's most far-reaching power is its capacity to set the public agenda—to determine what people will know, think, and talk about.[3]

As individuals we experience little of the world firsthand. We move in a small circle and do not observe directly much of what takes place outside our family, our neighborhood, and our community. For information about the world beyond, we depend on the media. Americans without work know the problems of unemployment only too well, but it takes the mass media to extend concern with unemployment to persons who still have jobs and who have no fear of being laid off. As Walter Lippmann stated more than fifty years ago, the mass media provide us with the pictures in our heads of the things that happen beyond our sight.[4]

The world that we have to deal with politically is out of reach, out of sight, out of mind. It has to be explored, reported, and imagined. Man is no Aristotelian god contemplating all existence at one glance. . . . Yet this same creature has invented ways of seeing what no naked eye could see, of hearing what no ear could hear, of weighing immense masses and infinitesimal ones, of counting and separating more items than he can individually remember. He is learning to see with his mind vast portions of the world that he could never see, touch, smell, hear, or remember. Gradually he makes for himself a trustworthy picture inside his head of the world beyond his reach.[5]

—*Walter Lippmann,* Public Opinion

To control what people will see and hear means to control the public's view of political reality.[6] By covering certain news events, by simply giving them space, the media signals the importance of these events to the citizenry. By not reporting other activities, the media hides portions of reality from everyone but the few people directly affected.

The difference is more than academic. Events and problems placed on the national agenda by the media excite public interest and become objects of government action. Those left off the agenda attract little public support and less political action. If the mass media ignores the problem of hunger, a good chance exists that a well-fed public and satisfied politicians will neither know nor care that many Americans need food.

The media's agenda-setting role affects the public's view of presidential elections. Through the media, voters not only discover what is happening in the campaign but also learn how much importance to attach to the things that do occur. This applies to events both on and off the campaign trail. No presidential campaign takes place in isolation. Each election is waged within the context of national and world events. The jungle trails of Vietnam were thousands of miles from the campaign trails of '68 and '72, but they were as critical as any word or action of the candidates.

The power to set the election agenda is the power to establish the context in which presidential candidates are evaluated. By hammering day after day at the issue of unemployment while saying nothing about busing, the mass media pushes unemployment to the top of the campaign agenda and shunts busing to the bottom. The effect can be decisive. An election fought over unemployment will be much different from one fought over busing. In some cases, even the final outcome can be altered.[7]

The network evening news plays a part in this agenda-setting process. Many Americans rely on network newscasts for their view of the political world, and their understanding of a campaign consists of the pictures provided by ABC, CBS, and NBC.

If public opinion is an accurate guide, television newscasts may even be the nation's leading campaign agenda-setter. Poll after poll has found that the public regards television's version of politics to be the most vivid and real. Almost half the people interviewed find television the "most believable" medium, with only a third citing newspapers.[8]

What is the picture that people obtain from watching ABC, CBS, and NBC? What do people come to know about, think about, talk about as a result of watching network news? What is the agenda that evening newscasts set in the public's mind?

The answer is disturbing: The legacy of network reporting during a presidential campaign is a television audience obsessed with election nonsense. What the viewer watches—the campaign trivia the networks so prominently display—is precisely how the viewer describes and defines the election world he cannot see with his own eyes.

Political Coverage in the Fall of 1972

Each evening on network newscasts during a presidential election, campaign reports take their place alongside other news stories. Some of these stories have no bearing on the campaign: the human tragedy of a plane crash, the devastation of a tornado, the outcome of a major sporting event. But others—reports of national and world developments, such as unemployment at home or war abroad—can have considerable campaign importance. They can call for government response and trigger candidate debate.

In 1972 the network evening newscasts were dominated by three events of major election importance: the campaign activities of the opposing candidates, the likelihood of a Vietnam peace settlement, and the possibility of widespread government corruption. Network emphasis on these three events was unambiguous. Some 54 percent of election-relevant network stories were directly about the campaign. About 16 percent were devoted to Vietnam peace efforts—the Paris talks, troop withdrawals, and the Nixon Administration's handling of the war. Roughly 14 percent touched on the topic of government corruption through discussion of the emerging Watergate incident, the Russian wheat deal, and the general theme of political misconduct. No other topic with implications for the campaign received more than cursory treatment.

As discussed earlier, network coverage of the campaign was limited primarily to its horse race aspects.

Network reports on the peace efforts in Paris and the corruption and crimes in Washington, however, were more serious in tone. The heavy network emphasis on Vietnam resulted from the intense coverage of the buildup and collapse of the October 1972 Vietnam peace settlement. In the early weeks of the campaign, Vietnam seemed a worn-out issue. Media discussion of the war was perfunctory. About five weeks before Election Day, however, the White House stated that progress was being made in Paris and that a peace settlement was near. The networks immediately intensified their coverage of the Paris meetings. Included in the coverage were almost daily reports on the government's actions, stories about the hush-hush bargaining and behind-the-scenes maneuvering, and outlines of the unconfirmed content of the proposed agreement. Optimistic reports continued, and on October 26 Henry Kissinger told the American public "peace is at hand." As the media began outlining the broad basics of the negotiated settlement, American troop withdrawal seemed imminent. Then just as suddenly as the optimism had been kindled, it was doused. Negotiations collapsed. On October 31, the Administration refused to sign the treaty, claiming the North Vietnamese had double-crossed them. McGovern, often critical of the progress and timing of these negotiations, immediately attacked Nixon's refusal to conclude the agreement and accused him of deceiving the American public and playing politics with the war.

Events played a similar role in network coverage of the corruption issue. Although, as the campaign wore on, George McGovern's speeches frequently sought to link Richard Nixon and the GOP to the Watergate break-in, the suspicious windfall profits surrounding the Soviet wheat deal, and the alleged favoritism shown ITT in its antitrust troubles, the networks did not rely on these attacks extensively for their coverage of political corruption. Instead, the networks primarily reported the events, background, and day-to-day disclosures associated with these charges—the grand jury proceedings on the seven Watergate burglars, the unsuccessful efforts of Democratic Congressman Wright Patman to hold Watergate hearings before the election, brief descriptions of investigative stories carried in the Washington *Post,* brief denials of the facts in these stories by Administration spokesmen, and reports from the Agriculture Department, commodity experts, and midwestern farmers on the circumstances surrounding the huge sale of American wheat to the Russians.

The Pictures in Our Heads

Few events in recent presidential history have been as serious and disastrous as Vietnam and Watergate. But viewers of television evening newscasts were not particularly mindful of these historical events. Instead, during the autumn of 1972, their political vision was dominated by campaign fanfare.

When recalling what they had seen about national politics on television evening news, 54 percent of the viewers mentioned a story about campaign hoopla—they described a candidate shaking hands, a partisan rally, the antics of hecklers, the results of a poll, or other kinds of political trivia (Table 1). Recall of such trivia completely overwhelmed audience recall of more important events—only 18 percent remembered a television report on the Paris peace talks or related events, only 18 percent recalled a news report about a campaign issue or some other substantive aspect of the election, and only six percent reported a story they had seen about Watergate or the Russian wheat deal.

What went through the viewers' minds provides clear testimony to the superficial agenda that network newscasts set for the American voter. A litany of what people remembered seeing on ABC, CBS, and NBC evening news reveals what the networks impress on their audience:[9]

There was this Nixon speech in Georgia. Don't remember what about, but they had the biggest crowd ever. More people seem to be getting out to see the campaign.

—54-year-old teacher

This guy was heckling McGovern. He was really heckling his speech. It was fun to see.

—41-year-old housewife

TABLE 1. VIEWERS' AND READERS' RECALL OF STORIES FROM NETWORK EVENING NEWSCASTS AND DAILY NEWSPAPERS (1972 ELECTION)

	Percentage of stories recalled by	
	Television Viewers	Newspaper Readers
Campaign hoopla (*e.g.*, rally, motorcade, polls, hecklers)	54%	31%
Campaign substance (*e.g.*, issue, policy, personal or leadership traits)	18	27
Vietnam peace efforts (*e.g.*, peace talks, Kissinger negotiations, troop withdrawals)	18	28
Corruption issue (*e.g.*, Watergate, Russian wheat deal)	6	7
Other events (*e.g.*, congressional action)	4	7
	100%	100%

NOTE: Data based on answers to these questions: *During the past few days, have you seen anything about national politics on television?* and *During the past few days, have you read anything about national politics in the newspaper?* Questions were asked of respondents in both early October and just before Election Day.

Vice-President Agnew was blowing that whistle. He was giving a speech for Nixon and instead of trying to talk louder than them, Agnew blew a whistle. He called them fascists. I thought the whistle was a cute little gimmick to quiet down the hecklers. It was a real show.

—44-year-old housewife

I saw McGovern and Shriver. They were getting off a plane from a meeting.

—26-year-old student

That Ted Kennedy really draws the crowds. You should have seen the people. He draws crowds that McGovern can't draw.

—32-year-old sales clerk

The candidates were out campaigning. McGovern and then Richard Nixon's daughter Tricia. They were on the campaign trail, shaking hands with people, and saying things, but I don't remember what.

—66-year-old laborer

I saw McGovern out campaigning. He was on the trail shaking hands. I've seen it before.

—67-year-old retiree

The President was in his car, and there were people lining the streets cheering him on.

—43-year-old businessman

There was this riot somewhere. Some guy poked a young kid. I don't know who was speaking. Maybe Nixon. [Writers' Note: Agnew was speaking.] I wish I could have seen more. I don't think it's right in politics, but I love to watch fights.

—48-year-old laborer

There was this crowd with George McGovern. It was a political rally. He got a good reception, that's what I remember.

—28-year-old secretary

Although the public is fascinated by election theater, the reactions of newspaper readers make it clear that minds filled with political trivia are not an inevitable consequence of media exposure during a presidential campaign (Table 1).

When recalling stories about national politics in the newspaper, only 31 percent of the readers cited a news report about election hoopla. Where more than half of the television audience recalls trivia, less than a third of the newspaper readers do. Nearly 70 percent of newspaper readers remembered a news story about important political matters—the substance of the election, the Vietnam peace efforts, political corruption, or some other significant public event. Quite clearly, the picture of the world established in people's minds by the newspaper was a more serious one than the picture provided by network evening newscasts.

If the mass media's most far-reaching power is its capacity to determine what people will know about and think about— in other words, to set the public agenda—then television network newscasts, during a presidential election, work to the detriment of a rational electorate. The networks do this because they make little effort, and have few available techniques, to distinguish the important from the unimportant, and because the most memorable pictures in this visual medium are more frequently associated with trivial stories than with significant events.

Surrendering Significance to a Fast-Paced Format

In its thirty minutes, network news presents many brief news stories. On a typical evening fifteen to twenty stories are broadcast. Each story averages slightly more than a minute in length, "frequently consisting of what would be the first two paragraphs in a newspaper story."[10]

The importance of a news story plays little part in its length. Truly extraordinary stories, when they first break, are given substantial news time, but coverage of even the most important events soon settles into the network pattern of 90-second reports. Most stories are about the same length, regardless of topic. During the 1972 general election, evening news stories averaged 91 seconds when the topic was campaign fanfare, 99 seconds when the topic was election substance, 95 seconds for the Vietnam peace effort, and 99 seconds for the corruption issue.

By cramming fifteen stories into a thirty-minute newscast (less the time for commercials) and making these stories almost equal in length, the networks render it difficult for viewers to distinguish readily one story from the next. If stories flash by rapidly and vary in length imperceptibly, then which story matters and which story does not? The viewer gains no clear-cut impression of a story's relative importance from network allocation of news time.

The brief time awarded each news story also means that the viewer cannot determine its importance on the basis of a thorough understanding of it. Usually, too little information is made available to convince the viewer of an event's significance. Events are frequently left to speak for themselves and seldom are augmented by in-depth reports, news analyses, or editorial comments. The headline-like reports on network news force viewers to go it alone, providing only raw information in the most superficial form. The result is that a story's significance is not fully impressed on viewers.[11]

Television's coverage of the Paris peace talks during the 1972 general election is a typical example. The peace effort was the major news event in the fall of 1972.[12] By no means, though, was it a simple event with an obvious outcome. It involved high-level negotiations, the comings and goings of prominent diplomats, sketchy indications that a breakthrough was imminent. Considerable background information and explanation was essential for a clear awareness of why these activities signified that American involvement in Vietnam might soon end. The network evening newscasts did not provide this kind of reporting. Almost every news story about the peace effort was merely a brief accounting of that day's activity and, by story length, indistinguishable from coverage of campaign fanfare. Vietnam peace stories averaged 89 seconds on the ABC evening news, 101 seconds on the CBS evening news, and 94 seconds on the NBC evening news. Campaign hoopla reports, by comparison, averaged 93 seconds on ABC, 91 seconds on CBS, and 88 seconds on NBC.

Perhaps, then, it is not too surprising that regular viewers of network news did not come away from their television sets, in the fall of 1972, thinking that the Vietnam peace effort was an especially important event. The same people were asked, at the start and end of the 1972 general election, the significance they attached to the Vietnam issue.[13] During this time period, those who were regular viewers were no more inclined than those who were not to attach increased importance to the issue. Interestingly, newspaper reading did influence people's beliefs about the importance of Vietnam. Regular readers did assign greater significance to the issue than people who did not pay close attention to the newspaper.

What explains this difference except the different news emphasis given to the Paris talks in the typical daily newspaper and on network news? The Paris talks were front-page news in the daily paper and emphasized by bold headlines and detailed reports. On the evening newscasts, the Paris talks were hardly distinguishable from news reports of campaign theater.

If they desired, ABC, CBS, and NBC could award appreciably more news time to significant ongoing events. On few days are there more than a handful of really compelling news events, and the networks almost always find room for light, amusing stories that are more soap opera, anecdote, and mini-theater than they are real news. But the networks have chosen not to exclude the amusing in order to explore the significant because to do so would bog down the pace of the show.

Television is show business. Television news is part of show business. As long as show business techniques can be used to convey information without distorting it, I believe it is perfectly all right. As a "show," a television news program requires pacing and style. Pacing, in my view, means letting the audience breathe a little between periods of high and intense excitement. A vivid pictorial report of battle action should be followed by an interlude of less exciting material. . . . Pacing can be achieved in a number of ways. The length of time on the air for (the anchorman) is one way. The length of time for the film and videotape reports is another. The frequency of switches from one man to another or from one film to another creates the sense of forward movement or pace. In my view, the audience has a very short attention span and it welcomes the change. . . . The result is that the audience never gets bored or finds its attention span taxed.[14]

—Av Westin, former Executive
Producer of ABC News

The motive for having fast-paced news programs, filled with the trivial as well as the important is exactly the same as the motive behind the network's emphasis on film. The networks want to keep viewers interested and entertained so that their newscasts attract the largest possible audiences. Lengthy, complicated news reports demand deep concentration and close attention, forcing the television audience to concentrate on absorbing the information and its significance. But work and television viewing are antithetical. Television, even television news, must be fun.[15]

The Power of Pictures

Television news has only one effective means of indicating the significance of the events it covers—film. By the use of dramatic pictures some events can forever be fixed in the viewer's mind. Who can forget the unsuccessful assassination of George Wallace in that Maryland parking lot or Jack Ruby taking the life of Lee Harvey Oswald?

The problem is that film is indiscriminate. Significant events do not always provide the best pictures; the best pictures are not always those of significant events. It is surprising how few news events lend themselves fully to the television camera. Many of the most important news stories come from "talking heads." Major governmental announcements, important international developments, the launching of new programs, the far-reaching decisions of individual political leaders, usually come in the form of the spoken and written word. Wars, mass demonstrations, and riots provide action film, but these events are not that common. Therefore, important events that provide good film are outnumbered by those that do not. Far too often, the most memorable pictures end up illustrating the least noteworthy stories.

It is also surprising to realize how often network pictures, despite the frequent claims that television news allows the audience to "see it like it is," do not provide true firsthand accounts of significant political events.[16] Often, a political event takes place unexpectedly, and the best network news can do is reconstruct it with after-action shots, interviews with participants, or staged re-creations. Other times, a political event, such as a court proceeding, congressional hearing, peace negotiation, or political caucus, occurs at a known place and time, but cannot be filmed because cameras are barred. When this happens, the networks film what they can, and then overlay their news story on the available footage.

Sometimes, these make-do pictures have little connection with the actual story.[17] Network coverage of the Paris peace talks is an example. As seen on television, this event often was negotiators stepping into their Citroëns or Lincolns, whisking through the streets of Paris; stopping at the site of the talks, disembarking with a wave, and walking into the building where the talks were being held. The narrative talked of important, high-level negotiations, but the pictures were light and motion. At times, the real significance of the peace talks was lost to television's theatrics, which had nothing to do with the substance of the negotiations. Instead of making the Paris talks seem all the more important, the available pictures often served to dilute them.

That news film is not always able to underscore accurately the importance of some major events becomes critical when it is realized that pictures dominate the television news viewer's recall. In television communication, the visual dimension overrides, sometimes even blots out the audio dimension. For most viewers, the pictures are likely to stand out while the words slip away. An analysis of the television audience's recall of 1972 campaign stories indicates that, fully half the time, their memory was primarily about something their eyes had seen. Only twenty percent of the time was viewers' recall clearly dominated by what their ears had heard.[18]

Therein lies part of the reason why the pictures in our heads that come from network news during a presidential campaign contain so little substance. Campaign hoopla may be mediocre journalism, but it provides action-filled pictures. Important campaign statements and coverage of domestic and international events sometimes provide less attention-grabbing film. A heckler being punched in the mouth leaves a more lasting impression than a candidate talking about inflation or Henry Kissinger assessing the peace negotiations or John Chancellor quoting the Washington *Post*'s revelations on Watergate.

A great irony about the mass media is that the so-called visual channel of communication—television—cannot normally give a powerful visual impression of significance. The newspaper has much more power to do so. Nothing on network news can match the newspaper headline for visual impact. Its placement and its size immediately cue the reader about the importance of an event:[19]

I read about the peace talks. It was on the front page that Kissinger and Nixon think the war will be over soon.
　　　　　　　　　　　　　　　　—23-year-old student

The headlines have been all about the chances for peace. The North Vietnamese have finally decided to sign.
　　　　　　　　　　　　　　　　—35-year-old housewife

It was on the front page. At last we can think about getting all the boys home. It's about time.
　　　　　　　　　　　　　　　　—54-year-old skilled worker

It is the print medium that gives its audience a strong, lasting, *visual* indication of importance. Network television news has no such ability.

When Television News Succeeds

Television news does not always make such a paltry contribution to the public agenda as it did during the autumn of 1972. It is easy to recall instances where the pictures in our heads can be traced unmistakably to the pictures on television. The civil rights confrontations in the early sixties, the riot-torn cities in the mid-sixties, the violent student-police confrontations in the late sixties, and the space shots and moon trips throughout the sixties are all instances where television news coverage left its own distinctive mark on the public mind.

But these are very special stories—each one satisfies very limiting conditions under which television news must operate in order to have audience impact.

First, television communication is at its best when it's broadcasting real, live events. No matter whether the event is the World Series, President Kennedy's assassination and funeral, or a political convention, television's most powerful coverage is live coverage. Because television news can take the viewer directly to the scene of an important event, it can enable him to participate, vicariously, in the making of history. When it does this, television news can attract and hold large, attentive audiences.

But more importantly, network coverage of such extraordinary, live events almost always preempts regular entertainment programming. This is television's unambiguous way of saying, "this story is extraordinary." It is television journalism's equivalent of the newspaper extra or the two-inch headline. When the networks want to indicate clearly a story's importance, their only totally reliable technique is to preempt regular programming.

Second, the pictures must be interesting, exciting, and tell much of the story. A man walking on the moon. Burning and looting. Demonstrators outside the White House. Viewers fix on the pictures and draw much of their meaning from what they see. For television to tell a story accurately and effectively, the pictures must be exciting, and they must be relevant.

Third, the story must seem uncomplicated and be easily understood. For this reason, television's big stories are usually tales of confrontation. Students against administrators, demonstrators challenging the establishment, black versus white. No one today understands this media principle better than George Wallace. As governor of Alabama he turned the complicated entanglement of civil rights and states rights into a simple televised confrontation—George Wallace standing in the schoolhouse door blocking the entry of blacks and their Justice Department escorts into the University of Alabama. Television covered Wallace's symbolic gesture live. Even though he lost the battle, almost everyone still remembers the pictures and the message. It was simple and direct communication by a shrewd manipulator of the picture power of television.

Fourth, television's coverage of the event or issue must be repeated regularly over a long period of time or must totally saturate shorter periods of time. Viewers are not easily impressed. Since learning takes place in bits and pieces, they must receive heavy exposure for the full impact to register.

Unlike the Paris peace talks and Watergate, one issue-event in 1972 lent itself perfectly to television news coverage—President Nixon's trip to China. Nixon's China trip was an intensely covered, live event. It was easily understood; its meaning was wrapped up in a handshake. News stories frequently interrupted regular entertainment programming to show the President and Premier Chou En-lai dining at a magnificent banquet in the Great Hall of the People. The pictures were mysterious, exciting, and informative. They were of a land and people most Americans had had no contact with for more than twenty years. Months later, during the election campaign, Sino-American relations were still an important topic. Almost universally, Republicans and Democrats, Nixon and McGovern voters alike, were persuaded of the China trip's significance. So on an issue of no immediate consequence to the bulk of the American people, television news, with a story ideally suited to the medium and with a week's saturation coverage, placed Sino-American relations high on the nation's political agenda.

Eventually, television news even had considerable impact on the public's conception of the Watergate-corruption issue. But only when network coverage began to conform to the necessary conditions. Throughout 1972 it was the Washington *Post* and the nation's newspapers that kept Administration crimes and corruption in the voters' minds. When the networks began broadcasting the Senate Watergate hearings, however, the issue became a television issue. Here again, the coverage was live. As an historically important event, it preempted regular programming. Although the story unraveled in these hearings was still bewildering, it began to be a good-guy, bad-guy confrontation. And the hearings were no one-shot event; they droned on and on. By the time of Richard Nixon's resignation, television news had contributed significantly to America's understanding of, and judgment about, Nixon Administration corruption.

But stories like these are few. Such events almost always receive "special events coverage" and are rarely confined exclusively to the nightly news broadcasts. So popular analysis of television news has made a simple mistake: Because television's coverage of certain events has a dramatic impact, it has been assumed *all* types of television news reporting have tremendous impact. Not true. Since the nightly news is too brief to treat fully the complexity of modern politics, too visual to present effectively most events, and too entertainment-minded to tell viewers much worth knowing, most network newscasts are neither very educational nor very powerful communicators.

PART II

TELEVISED POLITICAL ADVERTISING:
MEANINGFUL OR MANIPULATIVE?

Chapter 5
Packaging Presidential Candidates: Televised Political Commercials

VIDEO	AUDIO
Laughing teenagers bounding down road	California girls,
Girl in amusement park swing	Coney Island
Laughing teenagers bounding down road	beach,
	Rollin' on the river,
Kids playing hop-scotch	Dancin' in the
Laughing teenagers bounding down road	street,
Volleyball at the beach	Surfs up; Come on
	down,
Laughing teenagers bounding down road	Got so much to
Couple on merry-go-round	choose.
Young people jumping rope	Wouldn't let
	anyone
Boy surfing	stand in my
Boy putting on football helmet	shoes. . . .
Laughing teenagers bounding down road	Look up, America, see
	what we got. . . .
Teenagers galloping horses	(Voiceover) *We've got*
Young man water-skiing	*more things to do in*
Kids in go-carts	*this country than any*
	country in the
Kids in bumper cars	*world. . . .*
Tug-of-war at beach	
Young girl batting softball	

VIDEO	AUDIO
Youngsters playing basketball	We've got the real
Laughing teenagers bounding down road	thing. . . .
Boy chug-a-lugging a Coke	*And we've got the best*
	drink to go with
Couple drinking a Coke	*them.* . . .
Girl drinking a Coke	*The special drink*
Surfer drinking a Coke	*with*
	the taste that
Laughing teenagers bounding down road	*says.* . . .
in opposite direction	It's Coca-Cola. . . .
Three frosty bottles of Coca-Cola	*Look up,*
LOOK FOR THE REAL THINGS (Super-	*America.* . . .
imposed)	*Coke.*
	It's the real thing.

[30-Second Coca-Cola Commercial]

THE critics claim that the same advertising strategies and techniques that sell soft drinks also are used to sell Presidents. According to them, televised political ads contain several parts emotional gimmickry for each part useful information.[1]

But televised presidential advertising cannot be so simply stereotyped. Some presidential commercials that concentrate on symbols, postures, and slogans bear a striking resemblance to many commercials for nationally advertised brands. Other presidential ads are quite different. Using arguments that contrast sharply in content and style with the mindless appeals that sell some products, these televised political spots talk straight, and talk sense, to the American electorate.

Like every form of political rhetoric and persuasion, televised political advertising is schizophrenic. It has a face of illusion and a face of substance. Appeals from the former are shadowy, non-conflictual, and directed at people's sentiments. They create images and impressions. Appeals from the latter are concrete, consensual, and aimed at people's intellect. These arguments distinguish between the candidates, reveal the cleavages between the two, and build a case for one over the other. So political advertising is two-faced. It is neither all imagery, nor all reason, but a perplexing mixture of both.

One Side of Advertising: Imagery and Emotion

Presidential politics has always been a game of illusions. From the "Father of Our Country," to "Old Hickory" and "Tippecanoe and Tyler, Too," to "Honest Abe" and "Silent Cal," candidates have been described as greater men than they were. Their deeds and accomplishments, often commonplace, were magnified beyond any resemblance to their actual merits. Their character and virtues, often quite average, were enlarged and purified.

Campaigning in 1840

Oh, what has caused this great commotion—motion—
  motion—
All the Country through?
It is the ball that's rolling on
For Tippecanoe and Tyler, too
Yes, Tippecanoe and Tyler, too,
And with them we'll beat little Van—Van—Van—Van—
Oh, he's a used-up man.
Yes, with them we'll beat little Van.

Oh, let them talk about hard cider—cider—cider—
And log cabins, too.
It will only help to speed the ball
For Tippecanoe and Tyler, too
Yes, Tippecanoe and Tyler, too.
And with them we'll beat little Van—Van—Van—Van—
Oh, he's a used-up man.
Yes, with them we'll beat little Van.[2]

Not surprisingly, when televised advertising became part of the political stock in trade, it became another tool for making presidential candidates seem larger than life. Some observers have even contended that television, possessing among all forms of mass persuasion the greatest capacity for simulating reality, added a new dimension to this art of political illusion.[3] This belief that television projects unique images has gained widespread acceptance, as has the idea that television's images can be manipulated through the skillful use of the medium.[4] In turn, these assumptions have spawned a whole new breed of political middlemen, television specialists who attempt to build candidate images, just as the old-time partisan press and the traditional party hack helped mold the images of candidates past.

The 1972 presidential campaign is a typical case. Creating a favorable impression of the candidate's personal and leadership qualities was one of the purposes of the advertising efforts of both Nixon and McGovern. Since they came to the campaign by different routes, their image-making efforts were not identical. But the ultimate purpose—the image of a man suited to the presidency—was always the same.

Nixon's advertising imagery reflected his position as an incumbent President. He had a four-year record to build on. It was used to create the image of a farsighted, dedicated, active, and even historical leader. His ads were filled with the symbolism that only the presidency can provide: the meetings with world leaders in faraway places, the speeches on important occasions, the pomp and grandeur of the White House. The nation's triumphs during the four years of the first Nixon Administration became, in Nixon's advertising, his personal triumphs. Advances in medical science, greater cooperation between nations, economic growth, a better ecology, all were attributed to the vision of Richard Milhaus Nixon. And the public record was augmented with previously unseen film of Nixon. When the film was used in advertising, the viewers were told they were going to "glimpse the private man at work and in his relaxed moments, the man few people know." Richard Nixon was described as "a man of compassion, courage, and conscience." Because at that moment history seemed to demand so much, he was called a man that the nation could not do without: "That's why we need President Nixon. Now more than ever."

Excerpts of Imagery from 1972 Nixon Commercials

VIDEO	AUDIO
Ceremonies at airport as President Nixon and party depart from plane, review troops and greet their hosts	VOICEOVER: Moscow. May, 1972. Richard Nixon becomes the first American President ever to visit the Russian capital. . . .
President on Russian TV President laying wreath at cemetery in Leningrad Russian soldier weeping President leaving cemetery	NIXON: Yesterday, I laid a wreath at the cemetery which commemorates the brave people who died during the siege of Leningrad in World War II. At the cemetery, I saw the picture of a twelve-year-old girl. She was a beautiful child. Her name was Tanya. The pages of her diary tell the terrible story of war. In the simple words of a child, she wrote of the deaths of the members of her family. Zhenya in December. Grannie in January. Leka. Then Uncle Vasya. Then Uncle Lyosha. Then Mama and then the Savichevs. And then, finally, these words, the last words in her diary: "All are dead. Only Tanya is left." As we work toward a more peaceful world, let us think of Tanya and of the other Tanyas and their brothers and sisters everywhere. . . .

* * *

Picture of Nixon	VOICEOVER: The thirty-eighth President of the United States is Richard Nixon. Most of us see him only as a public figure. In this

VIDEO	AUDIO
	film we can glimpse the private man at work and in his relaxed moments, the man so few people know.
Nixon before audience at White House reception Nixon walks to piano Nixon sits at piano Nixon plays piano	NIXON: [applause] Now ladies and gentlemen. [laughter] Please don't go away. [laughter] Duke was asking earlier if I would play and I said I had never done so yet in the White House. But it did occur to me as I looked at the magnificent program that's prepared for us that one number was missing. You see this is his birthday. Now [audience laughter] Now Duke Ellington is ageless, but will you all stand and sing Happy Birthday to him, and please in the key of G. [laughter] [Everyone sings "Happy Birthday"]. . . .

* * *

Nixon speaking to aide in Oval Office	NIXON: What's the matter with these clowns. The whole purpose of this is to get property taxes down not to increase the budgets for local officials to continue to raise property taxes.
Aide speaking	AIDE: That's what I thought you'd say.
Nixon speaking to aide	NIXON: Unless you put the heat on these local officials they'll just take the money and pour it into all their pet projects and not get the progress of the collective interest. That's not the way it's going to be.

* * *

Nixon at state dinner in China	NIXON: I express my appreciation to my Chinese voice, to Mrs. Chung. I listened to her translation, she got every word right.

VIDEO	AUDIO
	[laughter and applause] [then Chinese translator begins translation]
Graphic: Nixon. Now more than ever.	VOICEOVER: Richard Nixon, a man of compassion, courage and conscience. A man America needs now more than ever.

The unifying theme of McGovern's advertising imagery was the simple slogan: "McGovern. For the People." The theme was played out in a series of political spots which showed him listening to the problems of the "common" people. He would discuss their situation and indicate that when he assumed the presidency he would create a government responsive to the needs of average Americans. Workers in factories, senior citizens in nursing homes, crippled war veterans in hospitals, these were the kind of symbols that marked McGovern's image-making. Always, the film showed him listening closely, talking intensely, sleeves rolled up and tie unloosened. Not only was he for the people, he was one of the people.

Excerpts of Imagery from 1972 McGovern Commercials

VIDEO	AUDIO
	MCGOVERN: Joel, were you with the Third Marines at. . . .
McGovern and veterans in a group	VOICEOVER: Most of them were still safe in grade school when this man first spoke out against the war—risking political suicide in the hope they might be spared. For them, his early voice has now been heard too late. If the shooting stopped tomorrow, they still have to face their long road back rebuilding shattered lives and broken dreams and are looking for all the help and understanding they can find. . . .

VIDEO	AUDIO
Close-up of veteran in wheelchair	ONE VETERAN: Why can't we get jobs in government offices right now, they should be the ones that would hire us first. They hire other people. There are people who have disabilities—stuck in these things—and they don't want to be here. Some of them can't use their arms and their fingers but that doesn't make them a nonproductive individual.
McGovern talking to wheelchaired veteran	MCGOVERN: You love your country, there's no question about that, and yet you're about half way mad at it too, aren't you. . . .

* * *

VIDEO	AUDIO
Open on McGovern seated with group of elderly women	FIRST WOMAN: We have people in wheelchairs, on crutches, and we need some kind of a facility where we don't have to sit helpless by and watch our neighbors die.
	SECOND WOMAN: They raise our rent, our food goes up, and we're back in the same position.
Cut to close-up of first woman	FIRST WOMAN: We're just being forgotten.
Cut to close-up of McGovern	MCGOVERN: You know, someday somebody is going to write the history of these times and I think it's going to be a pretty sad chapter when they write the story on the way we've treated our older people. And there isn't anything that we ought to want more than that those later years can be years of
Zoom out to shot of McGovern and group	confidence and security and decency, and I'm going to do everything I can to see that older people are treated decently. . . .

These attempts at political imagery bear a close resemblance to much televised product advertising. Nixon's and McGovern's image efforts were not quite as mindless, not quite as eye-catching, as the symbolism in soft-drink ads. But they were close. The difference in tone is largely a reflection of the more serious choice involved in selecting a President. The advertising experts who developed the Nixon and McGovern ad campaigns studiously avoided techniques that might make the commercials appear nonsensical. As one of them stated it: "We tried to stay away from what is known as Madison Avenue or product-show-biz type of commercials. Product ads can depend on singing, telling jokes, and all that. But you can't have that dominating advertising in a presidential campaign."[5]

In other ways, however, the parallels are striking. In its assumptions about people's behavior, in its manipulation of symbols, and even in its primary photography technique, the image content of political advertising is a near carbon copy of the appeals in product commercials. Both approaches aim at people's hearts more than their heads. Most product advertising is based on a simple assumption about consumer buying habits—people make purchases for emotional, not cerebral, reasons.[6] Efforts at candidate image-making rest on a similar assumption: The voter is "basically uninterested in making an *effort* to understand . . . emotions are more easily aroused, closer to the surface, more malleable . . . [the candidate] has to come across as a person larger than life, the stuff of legend. . . ."[7]

This assumption about human behavior dictates the content of much product advertising. It leads to a parade of symbols, flashing photographs, and easy-whistling music that try to associate "the real thing" with the happy times that call for an ice-cold soft drink. Political advertising follows the same practice for the same reasons. It tries to associate the candidate on an emotional level with the heartbreak of crippled veterans, the grandeur of the Oval Office, the tragedy of the victims at Leningrad, the plight of the elderly poor. By all these means, the commercial attempts to build an affective link between candidate and viewer.

Even the same photography technique—cinema verité, which means filming in natural setting—provides both product and political imagery. The Coca-Cola ad at the beginning of this chapter was a montage of vignettes obtained by cinema verité—people bounding down a road, kids playing hopscotch, teenagers galloping horses. The technique provides the most visually believable advertising, far more real looking than film produced in the studio or created on the graphics board. George McGovern found cinema verité a technique compatible with the illusions he was trying to create, and he used it extensively in his ads.

The critics are right, then, in claiming that some presidential advertising does little more than mimic product advertising. But they also are wrong about political imagery. They misjudged its origins. It did not begin with television. It began with politics.

The Other Side of Advertising: Issues and Reason

Amidst all of the elite concern, even horror, that some voters might pick a candidate in the same way that they buy a brand of soap, one aspect of televised political advertising has been ignored almost completely. Political commercials contain substantial information.

Spots contain many appeals designed to give voters solid reasons why they should support one candidate instead of the other. Most of these reasons come through issue appeals which, when delivered by commercials, take the same form that they always have: The candidate attempts to link himself with issue positions that he feels will win him votes and tries to associate his opponent with issue positions that will cost him votes. For example, a candidate who sees the public as strongly against forced busing to achieve racial integration may attempt to convince the voting public that he will put an end to busing and that his opponent will not. Prior to the use of television commercials, the pronouncements, position papers, and policy statements that emanated from a candidate's press staff to the news media for public dissemination represented the workings of that strategy. Such means are still used, but televised spots are also used. Of the political commercials televised during the 1972 general election, for example, 42 percent were primarily issue communications, and another 28 percent contained substantial issue material.[8]

As a result of this use of commercials, the total issue content of the Nixon and McGovern ad campaigns is impressive. Through McGovern's ads which appeared on television about one hundred times during the last six weeks of the campaign, and Nixon's spots which were shown nearly as often, some twelve policies were extensively aired (Table 1).

TABLE 1. COVERAGE OF CAMPAIGN ISSUES BY POLITICAL
SPOTS DURING 1972 GENERAL ELECTION

	Number of times mentioned	Total advertising time
Nixon policies:		
Vietnam	42	16:31
China	34	27:09
Russia	34	14:48
Inflation	34	11:00
Military spending	23	7:20
Corruption	20	10:58
Foreign commitments	10	8:29
McGovern policies:		
Military spending	37	17:23
Taxes	19	13:40
Vietnam withdrawal	16	9:10
Welfare	18	11:10
Unemployment	20	9:13
TOTALS	307	156:51

NOTE: Includes all references to these issues in televised political spots shown between September 18 and November 6, 1972, for hours of 7–11 P.M. EST.

Given coverage were an impressive array of foreign and domestic policies from Vietnam and China to taxes and welfare. Every one of the dozen issues received at least six minutes of television time, and more than half received more than 10 minutes of air time.

A comparison with network news' campaign coverage of the same issues helps put these advertising minutes into perspective. Of the twelve policies, *each* received more general election coverage through advertising time than through evening news time. During the period from September 18 to November 6, 1972, Nixon's foreign policies—Vietnam, China, Russia, and his commitments to America's allies—received more than 65 minutes of broadcast time in advertising and only about 15 minutes on the average network's evening newscasts. On the other Nixon issues—inflation, military spending, and corruption—advertising devoted more than 25 minutes of air time to them, and the evening news gave them less than 5 minutes. On the five major McGovern issues—military spending, taxes, Vietnam withdrawal, welfare, and unemployment—advertising devoted 60 minutes to them, while the evening news gave them only 10 minutes. Taken together, during the major portion of the 1972 general election campaign, these twelve issues received almost *five* times the air time via advertising as they did via the average network's weeknight newscasts.

Moreover, the twelve issues covered by advertising included many of the campaign's most crucial ones. Nixon's positive spots were strongly oriented toward foreign policy—emphasizing the administration's accomplishments and its commitment to an active role for the United States in world affairs. Nixon's negative spots criticized McGovern's military defense policy and his welfare proposals. McGovern's positive ads stressed Vietnam disengagement and domestic policies that would benefit working and lower-middle-class Americans—particularly tax reform and jobs. His negative ads attacked Nixon's Vietnam policy and his record on taxes, jobs, and inflation. Most certainly, the two candidates' advertising campaigns reflected what each felt should be the nation's policy priorities.

The issue appeals contained in political advertising bear little resemblance to the kind of product appeals typified by Coca-Cola ads. Where such product commercials are nonsensical, issue advertising is substantial. Where the product ad eschews conflict, the issue spot heightens it. Where the product message tends toward the soft sell, the issue message favors a harder sell. Where the product message simply tries to create awareness, the issue message tries to get the viewers to think.

Even the visual techniques of issue advertising are often quite different from those of mindless product advertising. Many issue appeals are face-to-camera ads, where the candidate speaks directly to the audience without visual aids. Some issue spots are even "crawls," nothing more than the words of the message on the screen while the announcer delivers the appeal. Neither technique serves the needs of much product advertising because they are considered too dull and visually uninteresting. When a candidate wants to reason with voters, however, these techniques have a place.

Excerpts of Issue Content from 1972
Nixon and McGovern Commercials

VIDEO	AUDIO
Close-up of John Connally	CONNALLY: Good evening. I'm John Connally. I'm a Democrat who along with many of my fellow Democrats has become convinced that it is in the best interest of this country to re-elect President Richard Nixon. . . . With this naïve view of the Kremlin, Senator McGovern has made proposals to cut an unprecedented thirty-two billion dollars' worth of men and weapons out of the United States defense budget. Let me show you precisely what he has recommended. If Sen-

VIDEO

AUDIO

ator McGovern has his way, the Marines would be cut by one-third. The number of Navy war ships would be cut in half. Our aircraft carrier fleet would be reduced from sixteen down to six. Fifty percent of our American fighter planes would be cut out of the Air Force. The McGovern defense budget is the most dangerous document ever seriously put forth by a presidential candidate in this century. It would end the United States' military leadership in the world; it would make us inferior in conventional and strategic weapons to the Soviets. The total United States armed forces level would be cut to a point lower than at the time of Pearl Harbor. Dean Rusk, Secretary of State in the Administration of John F. Kennedy and Lyndon Johnson, has termed the McGovern defense, and I quote him, "insane."

* * *

Script on the screen

VOICEOVER: When Mr. Nixon became President there were two million seven hundred thousand unemployed Americans, today there are four million seven hundred thousand unemployed. Since Mr. Nixon became President the nation has lost one hundred sixty billion dollars in national income through unemployment. Since Mr. Nixon became President the nation has lost forty-two billion dollars in income taxes through unemployment. Since Mr. Nixon became President four million people have gone on to welfare. In 1968, Mr. Nixon said: "What we need are not more millions on welfare rolls but more millions on payrolls." Mr. Nixon has spoken in favor of work but his actions have driven Americans by the tens

VIDEO	AUDIO
	of thousands into unemployment and onto welfare.
Graphic: McGovern —Democrat— For the People	VOICEOVER: McGovern. For the People.

But the preference in political commercials for content and substance is best emphasized by noting two opposing trends in television advertising. In the past decade, product commercials have become shorter. Market research has found that 20- and 30-second spots are about as effective as 60-second spots. Consequently since shorter commercials cost less than longer ones, there has been a marked shift toward the shorter message in product advertising. At the same time, presidential commercials have become longer. During presidential campaigns, the networks cut five minutes out of some of their prime-time entertainment programs and make this time available to the candidates for advertising. Presidential candidates have shown no reticence in producing five-minute commercials to fill these time slots. In 1972, these longer ads accounted for 41 percent of all commercials telecast by the candidates. Since each five-minute ad is substantially longer than its 60-second or 30-second counterpart, the portion of *total* advertising time taken up by these longer commercials is overwhelming—more than 75 percent of the total television air time consumed by presidential advertising in 1972 was through five-minute ads. In contrast, the 30-second spot was not a significant factor in 1972, accounting for only two percent of all ads shown and less than one percent of the total advertising time.

This obvious emphasis on lengthier political spots means that presidential ads can have more issue substance and more fully argued positions. In fact, several of the five-minute commercials used in the 1972 campaign would rival almost any newspaper campaign story, and overshadow virtually any television news campaign story, in the quantity and quality of its issue material. One such spot was devoted to John Connally presenting Richard Nixon's case against George McGovern on the issue of military spending. Although the commercial contained considerable political rhetoric and old-fashioned flag waving, it was a detailed argument of the Nixon defense posture and foreign affairs philosophy. Connally attacked McGovern for being naïve about foreign affairs and recounted Nixon's experience and accomplishments. Connally then sketched McGovern's proposed cuts in the defense budget and warned that the Democrat's proposals would severely undermine America's capacity to negotiate and its capacity to keep world peace.

Political spots, then, are not entirely the mindless creatures developed in advertising darkrooms that some observers have claimed them to be. Presidential advertising is instead a blend of soft imagery and hard issue material. The image content is intended to draw an emotional reaction. The issue content is intended to make voters think. In the past, commentary about televised political advertising has fixed on the image content, condemned it, and ignored the issue content. As the next two chapters will reveal, however, it is the issue content that is the far more significant in voters' reactions.

Chapter 6
The Impact of Televised Political Commercials

Television puts greater emphasis on, and it rewards in higher proportion, something that is not intrinsically related to political questions, and this is the production and merchandising of talent.[1]

Tom Wicker, New York Times *columnist*

The dominant goal of political broadcasts paid for by a political party is obviously the promotion of a candidate, not the enlightenment of the voter. This promotion takes its very worst form in the thirty-second or one-minute commercial where political issues are so oversimplified or ignored that the voter is given no information or, worse, misleading information.[2]

Elmer Lower, President, ABC News,
and Samuel L. Becker, political scientist

ONE minute after a product commercial fades from the television screen, most viewers have forgotten what was advertised. They cannot recall whether the ad trumpeted aspirin, shaving cream, or automobiles. A particularly clever or amusing commercial may draw some notice, and linger in their thoughts, but most product ads pass from the mind as quickly as from the screen.[3]

Presidential ads affect viewers differently. On television only a month or two every four years, their novelty attracts attention. Also their subject matter. They picture and discuss men seeking the nation's highest office, and most Americans feel that choosing a President deserves more consideration than selecting a brand of antacid. A clear indication of presidential advertising's attention-getting ability is that most viewers can rather fully recall the message of a presidential spot. When asked to describe a commercial they had seen during the 1972 election, 56 percent of the viewers gave a remarkably full and complete description of one, and only 21 percent were unable to recall anything at all from political ads.[4] In market research, any product whose commercials are recalled with half this accuracy is considered to have had a very successful advertising campaign.[5]

People also evaluate presidential advertising differently than product advertising. A study conducted for the American Association of Advertising Agencies in the 1960's discovered that television viewers judge product commercials more on *how* they communicate their message than on *what* they say about a product.[6] A commercial for a soft drink or a paper towel is regarded as good or bad by the television audience more on whether it is enjoyable to watch than on the truthfulness of its message or the value of the information it contains. People judge presidential ads, on the other hand, primarily on *what* they say, not *how* they say it. Whether the techniques used in presidential spots are visually appealing or unappealing seems to matter little. Viewers seem concerned mainly with whether the advertising message is truthful and worth knowing. Where the American Association of Advertising Agencies' study found that only 46 percent of viewer reactions to product ads related to the information communicated, 74 percent of viewer reactions to presidential commercials shown in 1972 centered on the information contained in the message.[7]

Thus, presidential spots get noticed, and the attention centers on the message. But to what end? Does the viewer learn anything about the candidates? Does he find out anything about the issues?

For years, most political observers have been certain they knew the answers: Advertising builds false political images and robs the American electorate of important issue information. On both counts, this orthodox view is wrong. In a presidential campaign, spot commercials do much more to educate the public about the issues than they do to manipulate the public about the candidates.

Advertising's Image Impact

In presidential politics, advertising image-making is a wasted effort. All the careful image planning—the coaching, the camera work, the calculated plea—counts for nothing. Just as with network news appearances, peoples's feelings about the candidate's politics—his party, past actions, and future policies—far outweigh the influence of televised commercials.[8]

Strong evidence for advertising's ineffectiveness comes from a look at *changes* in voters' images during the 1972 campaign. Just before presidential ads began appearing on television and again when the candidates' ad campaigns were concluding, the same people were asked to judge the images of Nixon and McGovern. They evaluated each candidate on seven traits associated with personality and leadership. Because the same people were questioned each time, an exact measure exists of how their images changed during the time when the candidates' ads were appearing on television.

These changes in voters' images indicate that advertising image-making had no effect (Table 1). Among people who preferred Nixon, his image showed a 35 percent improvement and McGovern's image a 28 percent decline. This happened among people exposed to many of the candidates' ads and to those seeing few commercials, if any. Among people backing McGovern, however, his image made a 20 percent improvement and Nixon's had an 18 percent decline. And

TABLE 1. THE IMPACT OF POLITICAL ADVERTISING EXPOSURE ON PEOPLE'S IMAGES OF NIXON AND McGOVERN DURING THE 1972 GENERAL ELECTION[9]

	Pro-Nixon voters		Pro-McGovern voters	
	Exposed to few spots %	Exposed to many spots %	Exposed to few spots %	Exposed to many spots %
Nixon's Image				
Experienced	40	77	30	44
Forward-looking	83	48	−14	22
Confidence-inspiring	46	65	−26	−22
Trustworthy	26	33	−50	−30
Appealing	14	27	−52	−29
Compassionate	18	−22	−22	−33
Not "political"	3	8	−17	−47
Average change	33	34	−22	−14
McGovern's Image				
Experienced	−11	−38	− 4	40
Forward-looking	− 3	− 6	14	45
Confidence-inspiring	−65	−47	16	− 5
Trustworthy	−33	−45	15	14
Appealing	−33	−12	24	21
Compassionate	−21	−12	12	20
Not "political"	−31	−30	45	27
Average change	−28	−27	18	23

NOTE: Figures represent percent improvement or percent decline (−) in people's images of the candidates during the 1972 general election. A full explanation of the figures is contained in Appendix D.

again, no significant difference occurred in the image changes of people heavily and lightly exposed to presidential advertising.

Thus, whether people watched television regularly, and constantly saw the advertised images of Nixon and McGovern, had no influence on their impressions of the two candidates. Whatever people were getting from political spots, it was not their images of the candidates.

As it did when examining the influence of network news on images, this conclusion gains significance from McGovern's candidacy. The South Dakota Senator was the classic little-known nominee. In his campaign, he depended heavily on televised political advertising, and in the vast majority of spots, he appeared on the screen to communicate his message directly to the viewers. If ever a valid test of advertising's image power existed, it was the McGovern campaign. His image should have become uniformly better or worse as a result of spot exposure. Yet, it became both better and worse, dependent solely on people's politics, not on their exposure to McGovern's advertising.

By projecting their political biases, people see in candidates' commercials pretty much what they want to see. Ads sponsored by the candidate who shares their politics get a good response. They like what he has to say. And they like him. Ads sponsored by the opposing candidate are viewed negatively. They object to what he says. And they object to him.

A sampling of viewers' reactions to the series of image commercials used by George McGovern throughout the general election campaign illustrates how strongly political bias affects viewers. These spots pictured McGovern among small groups of people in natural settings, discussing their problems and promising to help them if elected. The commercials were intended to project an image of McGovern as a man who cared about people. Whether viewers received this image, however, had little to with what happened on the television screen. It was all in their minds:[10]

He really cares what's happened to disabled vets. They told him how badly they've been treated and he listened. He will help them.

—37-year-old, pro-McGovern viewer

McGovern was talking with these disabled vets. He doesn't really care about them. He's just using them to get sympathy.

—33-year-old, pro-Nixon viewer

It was honest, down-to-earth. People were talking and he was listening.

—57-year-old, pro-McGovern viewer

Those commercials are so phoney. He doesn't care.

—45-year-old, pro-Nixon viewer

McGovern had his coat off and his tie was hanging down. It was so relaxed, and he seemed to really be concerned with those workers.

—31-year-old, pro-McGovern viewer

He is trying hard to look like one of the boys. You know, roll up the shirt sleeves and loosen the tie. It's just too much for me to take.

—49-year-old, pro-Nixon viewer

I have seen many ads where McGovern is talking to common people. You know, like workers and the elderly. He means what he says. He'll help them.

—22-year-old, pro-McGovern viewer

He's with all these groups of people. Always making promises. He's promising more than can be done. Can't do everything for everyone.

—41-year-old, pro-Nixon viewer

These people were watching the same George McGovern, listening to the same words, and yet they were receiving vastly different impressions of the Democratic presidential nominee.

Even undecided voters are not influenced by advertising image-making. Just like partisans, the candidate images of undecided voters fluctuate with vote choice, not advertising exposure.[11] In 1972, undecided voters' images changed very little and fit no definite pattern until *after* they had picked their candidate. Among those choosing Nixon, and only *after* they had done so, his image had a 35 percent improvement and McGovern's a 35 percent decline. This pattern of image change was the rule for those seeing many presidential ads and those seeing few or none. Likewise, for those picking McGovern, his image showed a 40 percent improvement and Nixon's a 55 percent decline. Again, there was no difference in this pattern based on the undecided voter's exposure to televised political commercials.[12]

Spot ads do not mold presidential images because voters are not easily misled. They recognize that advertising imagery is heavily laden with something that is not intrinsically related to personal character at all—how the candidate looks on camera. This pseudocharacter, to some extent coached, posed, and created by the best media talent money can buy, is a "look" built into spots that is totally unreal. And viewers recognize its meaninglessness. Even the candid portrayals of presidential aspirants that sometimes appear in image appeals are ineffective. People's guards go up when a spot goes on. So no matter the style of presentation, when only 60 seconds are used to say that a candidate is big enough to handle the presidency, voters find the message skimpy, debatable, and unconvincing. They know that the candidate will display his strengths and mask his weaknesses and that a 60-second glimpse does not provide much of an insight into a man's fitness for the nation's highest office.

Symbolic manipulation through televised political advertising simply does not work. Perhaps the overuse of symbols and stereotypes in product advertising has built up an immunity in the television audience. Perhaps the symbols and postures used in political advertising are such patently obvious attempts at manipulation that they appear more ridiculous than reliable. Whatever the precise reason, television viewers effectively protect themselves from manipulation by staged imagery.

Advertising's Issue Impact

But where image appeals fail, issue appeals work. Through commercials, presidential candidates actually inform the electorate. In fact, the contribution of advertising campaigns to voter knowledge is truly impressive.

During the 1972 presidential election, people who were heavily exposed to political spots became more informed about the candidates' issue positions (Table 2). On every sin-

TABLE 2. THE IMPACT OF POLITICAL ADVERTISING EXPOSURE ON PEOPLE'S ISSUE AWARENESS DURING 1972 GENERAL ELECTION

	Exposed to few spots %	Exposed to many spots %
Nixon's China policy	20	41
Nixon's Russia policy	25	29
McGovern's military spending position	45	66
Nixon's military spending position	20	33
McGovern's tax policy	18	33
Nixon's stance toward political corruption	15	19
Nixon's Vietnam policy	4	11
McGovern's stand on Vietnam withdrawal	48	52
Nixon's policy on foreign commitments	34	44
Average on all issues	25	36

NOTE: Figures represent percent increase in people's issue information during the 1972 general election. A full explanation of figures is contained in Appendix D.

gle issue emphasized in presidential commercials, persons with high exposure to television advertising showed a greater increase in knowledge than persons with low exposure. And on the typical issue, individuals who happened to see many commercials were nearly half again as likely to become more knowledgeable as people who saw few, if any, televised spots. Issue knowledge among people with considerable advertising exposure achieved a 36 percent increase compared with a 25 percent increase among those with minimal exposure. Persons heavily exposed to advertising were particularly aided in their knowledge about Nixon's position on China and military spending and about McGovern's position on military spending and taxes.

This information gain represents no small achievement. Televised political advertising has been widely maligned for saying nothing of consequence. Although the issue material contained in spots is incomplete and oversimplified, it also is abundant. So abundant in fact, that presidential advertising contributes to an informed electorate.

Advertising also educates voters because of the powerful way it transmits its issue content. Three basic advertising strategies—simplicity, repetition, and sight-sound coordination—combine to make presidential spots good communicators. Ads contain such simple messages that they leave almost no room for misunderstanding. Take, for example, the following McGovern commercial used late in the campaign to attack Nixon's handling of inflation:

VIDEO	AUDIO
Script of message moving up and off screen	VOICEOVER: Four years ago, Richard Nixon said, "we are on the road to recovery from the disease of runaway prices." Since Mr. Nixon became President, the cost of whole wheat bread has gone from 31 cents to 45 cents. Since Mr. Nixon became President, the price of hamburger has gone from 58 cents to 89 cents. Since Mr. Nixon became

VIDEO	AUDIO
	President, the cost of frozen fish has gone from 69 cents to $1.29 cents. Since Mr. Nixon became President, the cost of living has gone up 19 percent and your wages have been frozen. So the next time you are in a supermarket, ask yourself: Can you afford four more years of Mr. Nixon?
Graphic: McGovern— Democrat— for the people	VOICEOVER: McGovern. Democrat. For the people.

Ads deliver these obvious messages with a drumlike repetition. Spot messages are repeated again and again, as frequently as the candidate's budget permits. Research on product ads has found that with enough repetition even the most trivial and nonsensical messages can be imprinted on the audience. Anyone who has walked around humming a product jingle knows firsthand how right that research is. So it should come as no surprise that with all the repetition around election time even the details of political ads are learned by many viewers.[13]

> I saw this ad several times about how bad inflation was under Nixon. Bread had gone up from 30 cents to 50 cents, meat from 60 cents to over a dollar. It said that if Nixon was re-elected that things would continue to get worse.
> —47-year-old housewife

> There were these words on the screen telling how prices had gone up in the last four years. Bread was twice as much. It made you stop and think about what Nixon was costing us.
> —52-year-old factory worker

Moreover, political spots communicate their message through their coordinated use of pictures and audio. In advertising, viewers are not given the opportunity to draw one meaning from what they hear and another from what they see. Pictures and words are used jointly to drive home a single point. A graphic example of this is the following spot used by Nixon to attack McGovern's defense-spending proposals:

VIDEO	AUDIO
Toy soldiers, planes, and ships Portion of toy soldiers being swept off screen Portion of toy planes being swept off screen Portion of toy ships being swept off screen Script of Humphrey quote	VOICEOVER: The McGovern defense plan. He would cut the Marines by one third, the Air Force by one third. He'd cut Navy personnel by one fourth. He'd cut interceptor planes by one half, the Navy fleet by one half, and carriers from sixteen to six. Senator Hubert Humphrey has this to say about the McGovern proposal: "It isn't just cutting into the fat. It isn't just cutting into manpower. It's cutting into the very security of this country."
President aboard naval ship moving through the sea	President Nixon doesn't believe we should play games with our national security. He believes in a strong America to negotiate for peace from strength.
[Mandatory disclaimer]: Sponsored by Democrats for Nixon	VOICEOVER: Democrats for Nixon.

The value of carefully coordinating film and words is evident in the accuracy with which many people were able to recall this particular spot even several days after they had seen it:[14]

McGovern is going to cut the military. There were these model soldiers and planes and ships and, as the voice said, McGovern was going to cut the army by one third, the air force by one third, the navy by one third, these models were pushed aside.

—28-year-old office worker

It was about military defense and it had little soldiers and planes in it and the ad claimed that McGovern would weaken the armed forces, and that Nixon would not.

—56-year-old small-business man

Simplicity, repetition, and coordinated sight and sound combine to communicate effectively the issue messages of televised political ads. The value of this should not be dismissed lightly. For when a political commercial takes 60 seconds or five minutes to state clearly and directly how a candidate feels about a major campaign issue, the electorate is being helped to make a more informed choice on election day.

The Myth That Longer Is Better

Most political observers are highly critical of televised spots and wish that presidential candidates would forsake them for broadcasts at least 30 minutes long.[15] On its face, their argument appears reasonable. According to the critics, political spots are so short they reduce complex campaign issues to trivial and misleading nonsense. Therefore, since longer broadcasts permit more extended and meaningful political discussion, they are obviously preferable to the shorter political spots.

Does a series of spot announcements contribute as much to voters' knowledge of the issues and the candidates as longer programs where issues are discussed and candidates exposed to view? The answer is most certainly no.[16]

—20th Century Fund Commission on Campaign costs in an Electronic Era

---

The argument, however, has two flaws. First, and most important, it overlooks a crucial difference between advertising spots and longer broadcasts. People watch spots. Longer programs get turned off. Second, it exaggerates the consequences of commercial brevity.

A 30-minute political discussion must compete for an audience with other prime-time shows, and candidate-sponsored broadcasts are no match for television's entertainment programming. Faced with watching *All in the Family* or a half-hour political show, few Americans choose politics. Overwhelmingly, Archie Bunker would outpoll George McGovern. Just as overwhelmingly, he would outdraw George Wallace. Paid political broadcasts consistently wind up at the bottom of television's audience ratings. By their own admission, only one in twenty adults bothered to watch the typical 30-minute candidate broadcast during the 1972 election.[17] Regardless of how much information they contain, longer broadcasts cannot inform people who do not watch. A message unheard has to be a message unheeded.

Just as importantly, the people who watch these programs are more likely to be those who follow the campaign closely in the newspaper. Infrequent newspaper readers, precisely those people who usually are the least informed, are less likely to spend the time viewing a 30-minute broadcast—during the 1972 election, only one in thirty-five of these people watched the typical lengthy political telecast. For them, *any* entertainment program beats watching *any* presidential candidate for 30 minutes.

Longer broadcasts, because they attract only the highly partisan, have become the television equivalent of the traditional political rally. They are a gathering point for the faithful few, and a means for raising funds. (For a brief period after George McGovern's first 30-minute telecast, which contained a lengthy plea for financial help, small contributions to his campaign tripled.) But longer broadcasts are *not* the means to communicate with a cross section of the American electorate.

And finally, critics of commercial brevity exaggerate the comparison between the content in television spots and the content in other forms of political communication. Just because they may contain more words, do other forms of political communication contain more real content than political commercials? How many political messages in any medium outline an issue point-by-point, indicate the candidate's position, and then discuss whether the position is realistic, moral, and just. Almost none. It is seldom done at a campaign rally, in a direct-mail letter, or in the flyer stuck in the door. Regardless of the method of candidate communication, political argument is seldom academic dialogue.

Even when the candidate does not control the communication, political information usually flows, as Walter Lippmann described it, in bits and pieces.[18] Except in long magazine articles, lengthy pieces of newspaper analysis, or half-hour television broadcasts, issue information filters to the voters a little bit at a time. The typical newspaper story packs more issue material than a 60-second spot, but the 5-minute ad is a close rival. And without doubt, many 60-second spots contain as much relevant content as the basic issue blurb on network news. Indeed, the 5-minute ad is far more informative than almost any issue report on the nightly network news broadcasts.

Nor is it appropriate to evaluate advertising by looking at the contents of a single commercial. Any single spot is only one part of an entire ad campaign. Lumped together, the total advertising package of a presidential candidate contains a fair amount of information on a variety of issues, information which actually reaches millions of Americans over and over again. So in the final analysis, it is the short spot, not the 30-minute broadcast, that is able to have some cumulative effect on the broad electorate's sum total or political information.

Chapter 7
Do Political Commercials Manipulate the Uninformed Voter?

Politicians, with their advertising advisors, have discovered that the television audience is there and will not bother to turn off political spots. It is a group with weak political motivation and is not generally well informed. It does not care much for politics and for that reason will believe what it is told. The audience contains that group which makes its voting decisions very late. For all these reasons, it is this group to which the campaigns of persuasion are directed.[1]

—*Robert MacNeil,* The People Machine

The mass media campaign is not directed to the informed voter but to the eyes and ears of the voter who does not care very much.[2]

— *Dan Nimmo,* The Political Persuaders

ALTHOUGH a presidential campaign dominates the news for nearly a year, about one quarter of the electorate remains uninvolved and uninformed. These people find presidential politics so dull, complicated, and remote that they ignore it altogether. They take no interest in what the daily newspaper or network news says about the candidates. They certainly do not watch the party conventions. And through the entire campaign, they may never once talk about politics.[3]

At the opposite end of the spectrum are those people who are especially intrigued by presidential politics. Heavy consumers of campaign news, they regularly read about the candidates in newspapers, are likely to watch the conventions on television, frequently follow expert commentary in magazines, and occasionally talk politics with friends. At most, these avid campaign spectators constitute another 25 percent of the electorate.

The remaining voters—about two in four—are casual followers of the campaign. Motivated to pay attention more from a sense of citizen duty than a feeling of personal interest, these people, the most typical ones, pick up information in a hit or miss fashion. Somedays they may scan the newspaper or watch the evening news. Somedays not. They may watch an hour or two of the conventions. As likely, they will not. And in their everyday conversations, politics is a subject that rates only a passing comment.

In America, the mass media are so pervasive, however, that a little bit of campaign information rubs off on just about everyone, even the totally uninterested. But the varying attention that Americans give to presidential politics creates an electorate stratified in terms of knowledge. At the top stands a sizable minority well versed about the candidates and issues. Sitting in the middle are the majority of people who are modestly well informed. At the bottom is another sizable minority who are largely ignorant of electoral politics.

Informed or ignorant, however, these Americans share one characteristic—all of them are eligible to vote.

This situation has long perplexed proponents of free elections and popular government.[4] The democratic ideal is widespread electoral participation by a well-informed citizenry. But how can this be achieved when many people will not trouble themselves to become politically knowledgeable? In a democratic society, where people are free to determine their own pursuits, how do you get uninvolved, uninterested citizens to learn about politics?

The Unique Impact of Political Spots

To learn political information from the media, people must make some effort to seek it out. They must pick up the newspaper, purchase a magazine, or sit down to watch the evening news.

But televised political ads require no such effort. Ads seek out the individual. As people sit in front of their television sets in order to be entertained, commercials intrude with political information the viewer has made no effort to discover.

The audiences for these television entertainment programs are nearly a cross section of the American electorate.[5] As such, they include millions of politically uninvolved people who normally make little or no effort to learn about politics from the media. But when they watch television, the uninvolved get trapped. The political ad is sandwiched in the middle of their favorite television show, and it now takes more effort to avoid the commercial than to watch it. So the uninvolved watch, and they learn.

During the 1972 election, televised presidential commercials contributed heavily to the political education of the individuals who were least attentive to newspapers (Table 1). On seven of the nine election issues, low newspaper readers with high advertising exposure learned more about the candidates' positions. Only on Nixon's Vietnam policy, where they learned at the same rate, and on Nixon's policy toward the Soviet Union, where they learned less, did people who paid the least attention to newspapers not become better informed from seeing presidential ads. On the average issue, those seeing many ads had a 28 percent increase in issue awareness, whereas those exposed to few ads had only a 12 percent increase.

In fact, the effects of advertising centered almost entirely on people who ignored the newspaper. At best, regular newspaper readers learned very little from political commercials—those with high advertising exposure showed a 49 percent increase in issue information and those with low exposure showed a 46 percent increase. For these heavy readers, those who saw many ads learned more on only five of the nine issues. Occasional newspaper readers also learned very little from political commercials. Those seeing many political commercials had a 32 percent increase in information compared with a 27 percent increase among those seeing few spots. Here too, those with high advertising exposure had a greater increase in knowledge on only five of the nine issues.

Although it might seem paradoxical that spots would inform the less interested and simultaneously fail to aid the most interested, a ready explanation exists. The issue information communicated through the candidates' advertising campaigns was also available through the newspaper. For instance, McGovern's Vietnam and domestic policies and Nixon's foreign policies—the dominant themes of the 1972 advertising campaigns—were also recurring topics of newspaper coverage. Thus, people who were newspaper readers obtained the issue information without seeing televised political spots. On the other hand, individuals who seldom read their newspaper were likely to learn something new when they saw a political spot.

The result of this unusual learning pattern is that televised political spots act as information "boosters." They raise the level of information possessed by the less informed considerably higher than it would otherwise be.

This boosting effect touches every sector of the electorate. Every group has its share of people who give only passing attention to presidential campaign news coverage. But certain groups are less attentive and, as the average percent changes in issue awareness during the 1972 campaign reveal, these are the ones which benefit most from televised political advertising:

TABLE 1. THE IMPACT OF POLITICAL ADVERTISING EXPOSURE ON PEOPLE'S ISSUE AWARENESS DURING THE 1972 GENERAL ELECTION FOR LEVEL OF EXPOSURE TO NEWSPAPERS

	Seldom read paper %		Occasionally read paper %		Regularly read paper %	
	Exposed to few spots	Exposed to many spots	Exposed to few spots	Exposed to many spots	Exposed to few spots	Exposed to many spots
Nixon's China policy	13	24	14	28	41	76
Nixon's Russia policy	29	13	17	17	40	62
McGovern's military spending position	31	69	43	73	62	51
Nixon's military spending position	8	39	11	29	55	27
McGovern's tax policy	3	27	22	25	31	47
Nixon's stance toward political corruption	− 3	15	12	18	30	21
Nixon's Vietnam policy	−12	−12	24	11	8	28
McGovern's stand on Vietnam withdrawal	28	48	56	48	84	61
Nixon's policy on foreign commitments	13	29	41	40	60	71
Average on all issues	12	28	27	32	46	49

NOTE:
The same people were asked, at the start and end of the 1972 general election, where they thought the candidates stood on the issues. The percentages indicate whether people, during this time period, became more informed about where a candidate stood on a specific issue. A positive percentage means that more people became better informed about the candidate's stand. A negative percentage means that more people became less informed. A full explanation is contained in Appendix D.

	Exposed to few spots	Exposed to many spots
	%	%
Men	25	31
Women	24	34
Less than high school	5	24
High school graduate	16	34
More than high school	35	41
Income under $7,000	6	33
Income of $7,000–$13,999	36	26
Income $14,000 and over	32	44
30 years of age or under	16	33
31–59 years of age	27	34
60 years of age or over	18	32

Women learn more from spots than men because, as a rule, women pay less attention to political news. Traditional roles and experiences incline women to have less political interest, and, consequently, they spend less time following the campaign. The poorly educated gain more from spots than the well educated because, in general, they have fewer information skills, less civic interest, and pay less attention to the news media. Similarly, political ads contribute more to the information of lower-income Americans who, compared with higher-income persons, have fewer skills and less interest in political news coverage. Young people and senior citizens also profit disproportionately from advertising. Less involved in current events than the middle-aged, they make less effort to keep up with the news. All these categories of people—women, the poorly educated, the economically disadvantaged, the young and the elderly—have traditionally been less knowledgeable about politics.[6] In today's politics, however, advertising serves to narrow the information gap between them and their better-informed fellow citizens.

The Potential for Manipulation

Because television spots communicate so effectively with so many, they raise the specter of widespread voter manipulation. Although voters are not misled by the shallow and patently transparent image content of commercials, manipulation might still result from their viewing, and so easily accepting, the limited issue content of political advertising. Like all political rhetoric, on the stump, in the living room, in the union hall, or on the floor of Congress, political spots are full of small distortions. So brief they capture the merest shadows of the real political issues at stake and presenting these distortions to millions of voters with the 60-second certainty that only commercials can muster, the potential for manipulation seems truly extraordinary.

Not only does advertising fail to inform fully about any single issue, but it also fails to inform about the full range of election issues. Because the candidate totally controls the content of commercials, the viewer receives through political advertising only an approximation of the power struggle represented by a presidential election. Only those issues that a candidate thinks will help him or hurt his opponent are ever examined in his political spots. Many significant issues are purposely and systematically avoided because the content of political commercials is always determined by the candidate's desire to win elections and not by the voter's desire to make a wise political choice.

True, voters are afforded some protection against this selectivity. Although a candidate's commercials are entirely within his control, and say only what he wants them to say, the television audience is not the private preserve of a single candidate. Viewers heavily exposed to one candidate's appeals see plenty of what the opposition has to say. Since presidential advertising has not been timid about pointing out the opposition's weaknesses, some range of coverage is provided. But political spots represent a limited-issue domain.

So there can be no argument that in every presidential campaign millions of American voters are exposed through political advertising to distorted and limited information. In addition, this low-grade information is readily learned by a large percentage of the people exposed to it. And in many cases, the information learned from commercials ends up playing some part in their final vote choice.

But while all of this is true, the vast majority of Americans are immune to advertising's propaganda. They are not manipulated. And the reason is simple: They know too much; their views on politics are too clearly defined.

People who follow presidential politics closely through the news media are virtually untouchable. Not only do commercials seldom tell them anything new, but if they do absorb anything, it is overwhelmed by the other things they already know. The new tidbit of information simply becomes one of many factors that may affect their final vote choice. For these people, advertising may whet their appetite for election exposure; it may be a source of enjoyment or an object of derision, but it is not their basic source of vote guidance.[7]

Neither is advertising very important in the presidential voting of that broad spectrum of the electorate which, although not highly involved in politics, pays enough attention to be moderately well informed and has at least some commitment to a political party, a specific issue, or to some group, such as a labor union. Ads may contribute something to these people's information, but they seldom manipulate them. What these people learn from spots gets tested against their other information, and embraced or discarded depending on how well it fits. These Americans may not know their politics well, but they know it well enough.

Where the potential for advertising manipulation seems real is among the remaining voters—those people who virtually isolate themselves from campaign news coverage. For these Americans, if they watch and heed political spots, advertising contributes much of what they come to know about the candidates.

The Limits Of Hyperbole

Exaggeration is common in product commercials. Product advertising makes wild claims about curing ills, changing love lives, cleaning floors, and adding gusto to life. Hyperbole works much less well in political advertising. A clear example occurred in the 1972 campaign. Using a McGovern welfare proposal out of context, the Nixon ad campaign produced a spot entitled "Welfare." As the announcer claimed that the McGovern proposal would make half of the people in America eligible for welfare, the camera showed a construction worker on a girder high above a city, eating his lunch, and looking down on traffic in the street below. In the final seconds of the ad, the announcer said about McGovern's proposal: "And who's going to pay for this? Well, if you're not the one out of two people on welfare . . . *you* do!"

This commercial influenced few voters, including those without much information about politics. It pushed their credulity too far. People simply did not take the spot's message seriously:[8]

> Not even George McGovern is gonna put half the people in the country on welfare.
> —47-year-old poorly informed voter

> How can anyone believe that?
> —53-year-old poorly informed voter.

> That's just politics. They say the stupidest things. I wonder what they take us for. No one could believe that.
> —32-year-old poorly informed voter.

Some voters may have limited political knowledge, but they are not gullible. They are blessed with a healthy suspicion of the wild claims that come from politicians.

Some critics contend these Americans are easy targets for advertising rooted in demagoguery and deceit. Even making the snobbish assumption that uninformed voters are willing recipients of advertising that panders to prejudice and hate, political spots are too unselective to be a satisfactory vehicle for that kind of politics. To be effective, millions of Americans must see a political commercial, and its message must be palatable to a wide audience. So the "big lie" directed at the uninformed will also be seen by the more sophisticated. And these people will find it repulsive. The backlash will exceed the benefits.

In twenty-five years of televised campaigning, presidential advertising has been remarkably clean. Ads of a questionable nature, such as the famous "Daisy Girl" commercial used against Barry Goldwater in 1964, can be counted on one hand. And indeed in this case, public backlash caused the ad's immediate cancellation. Because commercials reach such vast audiences, their content must be carefully circumscribed. Indeed, the sordid museum of dirty politics in America has few exhibits of the televised spot compared to the numerous examples of the anonymous allegation, the whispered rumor, and the veiled promise to bigots in backrooms.

But what about advertising's "little lies"—its slight distortions, its selective appeals, its simplified messages? Do these manipulate the uninformed voter?

The Extent of Advertising Manipulation

Precise statistics on advertising's manipulative effects are hard to develop, because advertising, like other forms of media persuasion, works among and through a complex web of other influences. Seldom does a voter make his candidate choice for a single reason, whether the reason be political commercials, party loyalty, or a particular issue. Moreover, most people make up their minds about the candidates prior to the general election campaign, the time when presidential advertising saturates television programming. In 1972, as in previous elections where survey data have been gathered, about eighty percent of the electorate stayed with the choice it had decided upon before the general election began. Without doubt, some of these voters were reinforced in their initial vote choice by what they saw through television advertising. But how does one identify—among the people not changing their minds—those who would have changed their minds were it not for advertising? It is a treacherous task to assess whether people might have done something they did not do. So the effects of advertising on a voting decision are not that easily typed.

But some voters do decide their vote choice during a presidential general election and these people offer the best opportunity for understanding advertising's influence. In three interviews conducted with the same people during the 1972 general election, voters were asked which candidate they planned to support. If they changed their mind between one interview and the next, they were asked the reasons for the change and, if information about the candidates played some part in the change, where that information came from. By looking for advertising themes and sources in the reasons people gave for their vote changes, one way of estimating advertising's effects is provided.

This method of determining advertising's influence on people's votes has its weaknesses. Advertising has a "bad name" and, for that reason, people may be reluctant to admit its influence. To guard against this possibility, both the *reasons* people gave for their vote choice and the *source* they cited were examined. When people did not mention advertising, but gave a reason that clearly was a theme of the candidates' ad campaigns, their media use was carefully examined. If they were heavily exposed to advertising, the source of their vote choice was stipulated to be televised political advertising. Thus, advertising's impact is not likely to be underestimated significantly.

For three in every four people who arrived at their final vote choice during the 1972 general election, televised advertising had *no* discernible influence (Table 2). Some 42 per-

Table 2. POLITICAL SPOTS' INFLUENCE ON THOSE PEOPLE WHO CHANGED THEIR VOTE CHOICE DURING THE 1972 GENERAL ELECTION

	Percentage of vote changers %	Estimated percentage of all eligible voters %
No advertising Effect		
Choice influenced by events (*e.g.*, Vietnam peace talks, Watergate)	42	8
Choice influenced by interpersonal contact (*e.g.*, advice of husband or co-workers)	7	1
Choice influenced by party loyalty	11	2
Choice influenced by vague feeling (*e.g.*, "Don't change horses in midstream," "Time for a change.")	12	2
Choice influenced by no specific reason but person had little or no advertising exposure	5	1
Undetermined Advertising Effect		
Choice influenced by no specific reason and person had substantial advertising exposure	7	1
Choice influenced by advertising but choice was not manipulated	9	2
Choice influenced by advertising and choice was manipulated	7	1
	100	18

cent cited important events, such as the Paris peace talks, as the reason why they selected their candidate; 11 percent said they decided to follow party allegiance, as did the factory worker who said, "I've always been a Democrat and McGovern is the Democrat;" 12 percent gave an old maxim, such as "not changing horses" or "it's time for a change," as their reason; 7 percent said they made their choice on the advice of their spouse or a friend or a co-worker; and 5 percent, although unable to provide a specific reason for choosing a candidate, did not watch much, if any, television during the 1972 campaign. In all of these decisions, televised advertising may have played some part, but at most, it was only a contributory influence. Additionally, 7 percent of vote changers present the situation of undetermined advertising effect. These people could give no clear reason for their candidate choice, but they were widely exposed to political ads during the campaign. Televised advertising, then, might have been the reason for their choice although other explanations, such as party loyalty or important political events, are also plausible.

So the first fact that must be recognized is that political advertising competes with other influences for the loyalties of indecisive voters. Before televised spots were used, less-informed voters were choosing candidates because they had a vague feeling that it was time for a change, because their father had pulled the same party lever years before, because an event triggered a reaction, because their spouse or union leader told them what to do. Today, most indecisive voters still select their candidate for such reasons.

Clear cases of advertising influence occurred among only 16 percent of those people making their candidate choice during the general election, or roughly 3 percent of the total electorate, since only one in five voters make up their minds during this time. But not even all these people can be labeled the victims of advertising manipulation. Indeed, the second fact about advertising influence is that simply because spot information helps people make up their minds does not mean manipulation occurs. True manipulation through advertising involves more than voters obtaining information that subsequently guides their vote choice. Spots are truly manipulative only when they convince the voter to act in the candidate's best interests and not the voter's. By this definition, of the 16 percent influenced by advertising, about half (9 percent) *were not* manipulated and about half (7 percent) *were* manipulated. To distinguish between these two types of advertising influence, here are the brief, but actual, voting histories of two people who during the 1972 general election made their vote choice from advertising information.

The first voter is a 74-year-old woman, who before she retired worked at an unskilled job. In 1972, she was deeply concerned about having enough income to live on; her social security and small savings forced her to make ends meet on only $3,000 a year. Asked at the beginning of the campaign what one political problem troubled her most, she replied: "The amount of social security. It is not enough for most people to live on." Asked the same question at the end of the campaign, she said that "taxes were too high for older people on fixed incomes."

This woman called herself an Independent, but her past voting behavior had been strongly Democratic. She claimed to have backed Kennedy, Johnson, and Humphrey in the three previous presidential elections. Her choice for the 1972 Democratic nomination was George Wallace, and when McGovern got the nod, she was undecided about whether to vote for him or Nixon. In late October, she made her choice. She selected McGovern and gave this reason:

> I've seen many commercials where George McGovern wants to help older people, to get them more social security and otherwise help them all he could. Nixon has vetoed bills for helping older people and McGovern has shown a definite interest in doing something for us. If Nixon hasn't done anything in the last four years, he probably won't do it now. He looks after big business, not the worker. Nixon's funds are

from big business and they'll try to put him in again. I've no use for him.

The second voter is a 30-year-old hospital worker with two years of college. He is married and has one child. At the start of the general election, he was mainly concerned that the United States maintain a flexible foreign policy. At the campaign's end, he labeled unemployment the nation's major problem.

This man called himself a lukewarm Republican and in 1968 had not bothered to vote. But he registered to vote in 1972, and when the general election campaign began, he intended to support McGovern. By October, he had become undecided about McGovern, and just before election day he switched to Nixon. He cited one particular commercial as the major reason:

> I saw this ad where it says McGovern keeps changing his mind. It said he had first said this and then that. He did this last year and what about next year. It put a question in my mind about whether I wanted to vote for McGovern. He doesn't seem reliable as a person. He seems to be changeable with regard to the issues. So I eliminated him. Actually I guess Nixon has done okay the last four years. I'm not crazy about either one, but I'm voting for Nixon.

Advertising did not manipulate the first voter. It did the second. The woman used the best information available to her to maximize her political values. Although McGovern was making the same arguments about the elderly in his campaign speeches and they were more fully reported and criticized in newspaper reports, the woman did not depend heavily on the news media. But she received from advertising the information she most needed. It informed her about the candidates' social security and other old-age benefits, and she chose the candidate who promised to do her the most good.

The man, on the other hand, was manipulated. He responded to the candidate's interest, not his own. Through commercials, this man's view of his stake in the political system was replaced by the candidate's view. He was concerned about America's role in world affairs and unemployment, and yet he cast his vote on the basis of an idea placed in his head by advertising and seemingly unrelated to his own political concerns. He was used. He had no strong feelings that the nation needed decisive leadership and no firm ground for assuming McGovern would not provide it. His view of politics simply came to mimic the view of a Nixon advertisement.

America can tolerate the effect that advertising has on people like this man. Counting for one or perhaps two voters in every hundred that got to the polls, this man and others like him will select a candidate for trivial reasons with or without advertising. (Before being persuaded by the Nixon commercial, the man indicated his vote for McGovern was premised on the fact that "McGovern had got a raw deal because of all the criticism about Eagleton.") And besides, since their reasons for choosing a candidate seem randomly selected, their votes distribute about equally between the candidates.

The benefits provided other voters by televised political advertising far exceed this kind of cost. Not only do more Americans, like the woman who learned which candidate was best for her, obtain information that helps them determine how their self-interest can be served, but many more people acquire information that helps them to validate a prior decision. And then there are people who simply learn a little more from ads than what they would have otherwise been able to learn.

As inconceivable as it may seem to some, political advertising provides many less-knowledgeable voters with the most systematic, general information they will possess about the candidates. In 1972, for example, the advertising campaigns of Richard Nixon and George McGovern provided a reasonably accurate composite of the candidates' policy priorities and commitments. A somewhat attentive viewer, who saw many of the candidates' spots, would have come to the realization that Nixon was most concerned and active in foreign affairs, while McGovern, beyond his opposition to the Vietnam war, was committed to domestic programs that would make the economic system more responsive to the needs of people in the working and lower-middle classes. This information would appear to have been reliable and useful for people who previously were unaware of it or did not have it clear in their minds.

To be sure, advertising's information is not rich in nuances, and the candidates' issue statements are not provided much context. The keen understanding of issues that can come from close, continual attention to the newspaper will not come from seeing political spots. But this shortcoming has little relevance to the decisions made by uninformed citizens. Their rationality, when it exists, is narrow. It depends much less on what is happening "out there" than on what is happening to them personally. The context of their vote is furnished by the status of their own lives, not the state of the world. For these people, the information in ads is better than no information at all. And the weakness of ads is that they are not more abundant and inclusive, covering a wider range of issues more heavily. Only then would these people be relatively certain of getting the particular piece of information they need.

PART III

TELEVISED PRESIDENTIAL POLITICS: RIGHTING SOME WRONGS

Chapter 8
Responsible Journalism and Rational Candidates

The making of a televised campaign report is three parts television technique and one part political journalism.[1]
—*Timothy Crouse, journalist and author of* The Boys on the Bus

If politicians perceive the electorate as responsive to father images, they will give it father images. If they see voters as most certainly responsive to nonsense, they will give them nonsense. If they see voters as susceptible to delusion, they will delude them. If they see an electorate receptive to the cold, hard realities, they will give it the cold, hard realities . . . voters are not fools. To be sure, many individual voters act in odd ways indeed; yet in the large the electorate behaves about as rationally and responsibly as we should expect, given the clarity of the alternatives presented to it and the character of the information available to it. In American presidential campaigns of recent decades the portrait of the American electorate that develops from the data is not one of an electorate straitjacketed by social determinants or moved by subconscious urges triggered by devilishly skillful propagandists. It is rather one of an electorate moved by concern about central and relevant questions of public policy, of governmental performance, and of executive personality.[2]
—*V. O. Key, Jr.,* The Responsible Electorate

THE problem with television's entry into national politics is that network news departments and presidential candidates consistently misuse the medium and underrate their audiences.

Primarily because network campaign news contains so little meaningful information, it fails to have any meaningful effect on the viewers' feelings about the candidates and knowledge of the issues. Television's only effect on the American voter is to cheapen his conception of the campaign process and to stuff his head full of nonsense and trivia.

The networks could not maintain this charade without the active cooperation of presidential candidates who tailor their campaigns to every dictate of the television camera.

The networks broadcast the pap and the candidates agree to provide it because both believe the myths about the power of television and because both have a false conception of the capacities and expectations of the American voter. The networks' appeals to viewers, and the candidates' appeals to voters, are premised on a low regard for the basic good sense and intelligence of the public. The result is that the electorate is deprived of vital information; the networks fail to live up to the standards of responsible journalism; and the candidates, in addition to cheating the voters of a meaningful choice, cheat themselves by acting in a manner unlikely to persuade even the most uninformed and uninterested voter.

The Network Defense: A Frail Argument

The networks contend that they are acting responsibly. Television news says repeatedly "that it does operate in the public interest because it gives the public 'what it wants'."[3] According to the standard network argument, the viewing audience demands good pictures and a snappy format, even at the cost of informative news coverage. And by responding to this demand, the networks feel they meet their public obligation. (A corollary is the networks' fear that, if they fail to furnish such news coverage, much of their audience and the advertising revenue that accompanies it will be lost.)

You know, newspaper publishers take popularity ratings too. The answers are pretty clear; it is almost always the comics, followed by the advice-to-the-lovelorn columns. But, ladies and gentlemen, the news is still on the front page of all newspapers, the editorials are not replaced by more comics, the newspapers have not become one long collection of advice to the lovelorn.[4]

—*Newton Minow, former Chairman of the FCC, in a speech to the National Association of Broadcasters*

The network argument has two flaws. First, it fails to acknowledge the news media's traditional role in informing the electorate. No amount of evidence that the public is satisfied with network election coverage can hide the media's obligation for serving as a public educator. If television news is obsessed with campaign hijinks; if it does not consider careful reporting of the candidates and issues as its primary task; if it is not concerned with searching for significance, then television network news is not living up to its Fourth Estate responsibilities. The news must be more than a source of revenue. It must also serve the serious needs of a democratic society.

A second flaw in the network argument is that no solid evidence exists for the contention that the viewing public must be treated to an unending reel of dramatic film or it will stop watching the news. Although many observers other than network news personnel believe this, it is not an established fact that the size of the *national* news audience actually depends directly on the proportion of exciting pictures contained in a given broadcast. First, no reliable studies have been conducted to determine exactly what the viewing audience will tolerate in network news presentations.[5] Second, the networks have never really experimented with their format in the market place to discover the limits of public toleration. From inception, the networks have had a policy of action pictures at the expense of informative reporting. From inception, and harking back to the breathless shouting days of radio news, the networks have given the viewers just the headlines in order to make the news breeze along.[6] So when they claim that the public insists on this shoddy journalism, the networks are merely endorsing the only television news product the American people have been offered.

Some observers point to the obvious success of certain local affiliates, which have abandoned any pretense of serious journalism, as proof that entertainment, not information, attracts news viewers. These "happy time" local newscasts are glutted with easy bantering, sheer sensationalism, and outright clowning, and they attract large audiences. But do people have the same expectations for network *national* news as they do for *local* news, weather, and sports? Probably not. At least none of the networks have been willing to risk their present audience, or their journalistic reputations, to find out whether a total entertainment orientation would lead to an even greater national audience.

In defending their news practices, the networks themselves have pointed more to the lack of audience interest in prime-time documentaries. News documentaries do not draw large audiences, and the networks have often claimed that this "proves" that most viewers are not interested in *any* serious television journalism.

This facile conclusion is also troublesome. It is problematic because people do not see all "news" in the same way. There is "daily" news that tells them what is happening in the world. And there is "other" news that provides in-depth looks at special topics. Their interest in "other" news is not a suitable basis for judging their likely reactions to "daily" news. Consider the newspaper reader as an example. The reader is not deterred by the serious journalism that he finds on the front page. In fact, many more Americans read the front page of a newspaper than watch the nightly news. But it is also clear that only a small portion of newspaper readers trouble themselves with the serious journalism of in-depth newspaper stories. Should the newspaper editor take this fact as a mandate to eliminate serious journalism from the front page? Of course not. Reasons quite beyond the seriousness of the journalism account for people's lack of interest in either special, in-depth newspaper stories or special television news documentaries. This news material, by definition, is likely to appeal only to those few people who are particularly interested in the topic. "Daily" news has a wider market. Further, television viewers have different expectations during the dinner hour than during prime-time hours. To watch television in prime time is to expect and seek entertainment, not information from news documentaries. To watch during the dinner hour is to expect the "daily" news.

When it comes to this daily news, people will accept it in the form of serious journalism, or in the form of not-so-serious journalism. More than to be entertained, they want to satisfy their simple desire "to find out what's happening." They will take what they get.

Now certainly, the television news audience expects a visual presentation of the news, and networks face audience problems that newspapers do not. Some people without any interest in the news leave on their television sets. Although good pictures may be about the only thing that occasionally attracts the attention of such viewers, they are a distinct minority. Most viewers watch to "get the news," and it is doubtful they notice which nights provide better pictures. It is much more likely they notice when the news events themselves are dull.

Moreover, most Americans do not even care which network provides their daily news. The best predictor of audience size for any network nightly newscast is the audience size for the program that precedes it. In those locations where ABC's pre-news programs have the most viewers, ABC Evening News draws the biggest audience. The same holds true for CBS and NBC. This tendency is the well-documented influence of "audience flow"—the tendency for most television programs to inherit many of their viewers from the preceding show.[7] *All in the Family* may inspire many viewers to switch a given channel, but network news does not. Some people, out of habit or because they like a particular anchorman, may prefer one network's newscast over the others, but the bulk of the viewing audience does not shop between the networks to determine which newscast is likely to provide the most exciting pictures and snappiest format.

It seems clear: The networks have more freedom to practice responsible journalism than they have granted themselves. There is room for change. Perhaps not for fundamental change, since viewers do expect to see the news in film and expect all of the day's major stories to be reported. But these audience expectations may be rather flexible. Would viewers notice the difference if, most evenings, only 8 or 10 stories rather than 15 or 20 were carried? Would they perceive a change if slightly less news film were used and if that film contained a greater portion of "talking heads" and less action? It seems unlikely.

At the least, networks could alter the portion of their newscasts that every fourth year is granted to coverage of the presidential campaign. These national elections are special opportunities for network television news. As a news medium that reaches the entire nation, network television cannot cover election contests at the state and local level with enough frequency or depth to inform those constituencies. For those races, the local newspaper carries the democratic responsibility to keep the public informed. But at the presidential level, network news can and should meet its obligations to the electorate. The networks even have the advantage that during presidential campaigns the voters are more attentive to political information than at any other time.

In making this contribution, the networks might simply substitute more news stories on the candidates' qualifications and issue positions for news reports based on campaign hoopla. It can be said, however, that these stories would be too brief and fleeting to be very informative. Candidates' records, their abilities, and their policies are not easily absorbed by the eye and ear when they fly past in a news mix involving nearly a score of stories.

So during presidential elections, the networks would provide a more valuable service if they set aside up to 10 minutes each night for in-depth comparisons of the candidates on important issues or leadership dimensions. These stories might involve several types of news presentation: a simple statement of what is to be examined; an exposition of the background, using available film and visual material; and an analysis through informed commentary, using guest commentators if the networks' personnel lacked the necessary expertise.[8] Such reports would be a significant step toward changing network election coverage for the better.

One network tried a similar approach during the last week of the 1972 campaign. Using imaginative graphics and existing film footage, CBS Evening News presented a few lengthy reports on the election issues. These reports were a clear departure from what the networks usually do as, point-by-point, Walter Cronkite explained the different positions of Nixon and McGovern on several major issues.[9] If the nightly newscasts of ABC, CBS, and NBC are to contribute substantially to the electorate's information about the candidates and issues, however, reports like the one on CBS would have to be a regular feature of their election coverage.

How would television viewers react to more serious election journalism? The odds at least favor their *passive* acceptance of it. For one thing, viewers have no real enthusiasm for the manner in which presidential campaigns are covered now. Each night seems like a rerun of the night before. About sixty percent of all network reports that contain film of a presidential candidate picture him at an election rally, surrounded by a huge crowd. The city changes—one evening it is Minneapolis, the next it is St. Louis, then Portland, and around the continental merry-go-round. On camera, however, each rally looks very much the same, and viewers come to find it all very boring:[10]

> It's the same thing every night. The candidate out shaking hands. I'm tired of it.
>
> —31-year-old sales clerk

> Saw the same thing last night that I see every night. George McGovern at one of those rallies.
>
> —53-year-old factory worker

> It's so repetitious. I don't pay any attention any more.
>
> —42-year-old housewife

> Once you see one of those things [election rallies], you've seen them all.
>
> —44-year-old craftsman

And when questioned more systematically, most people indicate a desire for election reports that, in effect, would make campaign coverage more informative. Although the networks assume that viewers want campaign action, not substance, because the first is entertaining and the second is boring, people's preferences reveal no such demand. By six to one, people said they want to see *fewer* network reports showing the "candidates moving through crowds of people." By two to one, people indicated a desire for *fewer* reports picturing the "candidates speaking at political rallies." In contrast, people claimed, by three to one, that they want *more* stories showing the "candidates being interviewed by reporters." And by two to one, people expressed a preference for *more* reports in which experts and voters were pictured "talking about the candidates."

Evidence such as this must be interpreted with care. In the past, what people have said they want from television and what they have actually watched have sometimes been quite different. In truth, people's preferences in election reporting may say more about how the voters feel a campaign should be reported than what they would actually prefer to watch. The public understands fully what presidential elections are supposed to be. The American voter knows that the ideal election is one where the issues are made clear and the candidates are subject to scrutiny. It is this sentiment, as much as people's viewing "tastes," that is represented in their news preferences.

Television networks could try to appeal to this higher instinct in the American voter. Exciting campaign pictures may or may not be the lowest common denominator for the television election audience, but at least the audience knows it should want more. To date, however, journalistic responsibility and the democratic ideal have lost out to the networks' low opinion of the typical news viewer.

The Candidate and Television:
Pursuing an Unwise Strategy

It is a fitting irony that patently meaningless television imagery fails to convince the American electorate. Presidential candidates' self-interest, as well as the nation's best interest, would be better served by television campaigns based on political substance.

Believability is the first requirement for effective media propaganda. Voters must accept what is being said; the message must become part of their thinking about the candidate. It is quite true that to accept a candidate's message is not always to be persuaded by it. A voter may change his thinking about a candidate and still vote against him. But message acceptance is a necessary first step on the road to winning votes.

Television image-making fails to make it past the believability barrier. Television style and superficial mannerisms leave no impression with viewers about a candidate's fitness for the presidency. Voters simply fail to get the message that empty imagery is contrived to convey.

A candidate's issue positions, however, do get past this obstacle. They can be communicated effectively. Even people who intend to vote for his opponent get the message when a candidate makes clear his stand on important policy questions. Equally well communicated through the mass media are a candidate's group commitments, his personal record, his past accomplishments, and his personal background. The reason why these messages register with the electorate is that they are, for the most part, factual. And several decades of media research have demonstrated that "facts" get communicated.[11]

What does it gain a candidate, however, to build his media campaign around issues, his group commitments, and his personal and political history? George McGovern and Barry Goldwater tried that, and they lost nearly every state in the Union. So conventional political wisdom suggests that speaking too loudly and too clearly on the issues is a strategy for defeat.

But observers have misinterpreted these ruinous candidacies and have ignored other evidence—well-documented in careful research conducted by political scientists—that the electorate is becoming increasingly responsive to issues.[12] This same research would say that the candidacies of Goldwater and McGovern fell apart, not because issues were prominent, but because many of their issue proposals were poorly conceived and totally unwanted by overwhelming majorities of voters. The proper lesson from the Goldwater and McGovern defeats is not that issues make poor propaganda but that, because voters are increasingly concerned about issues, a candidate who advocates what most voters oppose is in serious trouble. If issues did not matter, neither Goldwater nor McGovern would have been so decisively whipped.

By comparison, if the thinking behind television image-making was correct, Goldwater and McGovern would have fared well. Each candidate was more photogenic and had a "cooler" personality, in the McLuhan sense, than his opponent. At their engineered-for-television rallies, each candidate drew more enthusiasm from his followers than did his opponent. Operating on assumptions about television imagery, it was Johnson and Nixon who should have been in trouble.

Voters simply are not fools. Some individuals do choose their candidate for strange reasons. But most of the electorate is "moved by concern about central and relevant questions of public policy, of governmental performance, and of executive personality."[13] Issues and candidates' qualifications also are the focus of people's attention to the campaign.

Because the bulk of the electorate can separate wheat from chaff, few citizens are interested in campaign rallies and candidate motorcades. Consider this list of reasons why people say they pay attention to a political campaign. "Excitement" is last on the list.

Percent Agreeing

To judge what presidential candidates are really like.	60%
To help me make up my mind who to vote for.	59%
To see what each presidential candidate would do if elected.	53%
To keep up with the main issues of the day.	53%
To see what presidential candidates would do for people like me.	51%
To remind me of the strong points of the presidential candidate I support.	38%
To get information to talk politics with others.	27%
To judge which presidential candidate is likely to win the election.	18%
To enjoy the excitement of a presidential election.	16%

Candidates have assumed that people are bored by issues and hard facts about their qualifications and that they find imagery and hoopla both more interesting and more persuasive. Candidates simply have been wrong in this judgment.

A media campaign where issues and candidate character are the themes can work. However, it must be the right kind of media campaign.

Both Goldwater and McGovern faltered by selecting the unsuccessful strategy of *opinion persuasion*. They adopted issue positions favored by a minority of the public and then tried to convince the bulk of the people that the minority position was preferable. Efforts such as those are certain to fail. A presidential campaign is no place to change people's opinions and values. Much evidence documents that, when people are in the midst of overt attempts to persuade and propagandize, they protect themselves. Their psychological barriers against manipulation are mobilized. They are wary, and their more cherished opinions cannot be altered. Opinion persuasion simply will not work in the charged atmosphere of a presidential campaign.

Substantive campaigns can win votes, however, through *information persuasion*.[14] Information persuasion is the process of altering people's views of a candidate by providing them information ("facts") that change their perceptions of the candidate rather than trying to change their own stands on the issues. Consider a candidate who has been a firm advocate of busing. He cannot persuade people who oppose busing to believe that busing is good. Nor can he say that he has had a change of heart and is now against this means of school integration. Voters would be suspicious of such an appeal occurring during the heat of the campaign. But the candidate's media propaganda, provided his past record makes it plausible, can state and state again his commitment to a strong military defense. Most voters will accept his commitment as valid, and this information will expand their store of knowledge about him. The candidate will still be seen in the voters' eyes as probusing, but now they will also consider him a firm advocate of defense preparedness. If the candidate can further persuade voters that a strong defense is a more compelling national concern than forced busing, and something a President can do more about, he has made an inroad toward picking up votes.

A second illustration may further clarify information persuasion. Take a candidate whose political activity has always been strongly probusiness. Media appeals that declare his support for the working man will fail. Contrary information overwhelms any such obvious propaganda. Nor will he be able to convert people with antibusiness attitudes to his probusiness position. But campaign messages that document the candidate's ability to get important legislation through Congress will be believed by most voters, if the evidence is clear. The candidate will still be seen as probusiness, but voters will also regard him as a politician who can get things accomplished. By getting them to regard this capacity as a very important element in the execution of the presidency, the candidate will have begun the process of winning votes.

Although oversimplified, the examples suggest why information persuasion is the only reasonable objective of media appeals in a presidential campaign. First, it involves the communication of material that people will accept. The candidate cannot be served by media messages that do not register in voters' minds. Second, it operates within the framework established by existing public opinion and merely attempts to link the candidate with political positions and abilities that voters think are desirable. After establishing that linkage, it works to convince voters that this new information should play an important part in their final candidate evaluations. No attempt is ever made to change resistant attitudes.

Today, in the past, and for the foreseeable future, the real persuasive message is what the candidate stands for. One of the more mischievous beliefs to gain hold on the minds of presidential candidates has been Marshall McLuhan's dictum that the medium is the message. Maybe over long periods of time and in subtle ways, the television medium has altered the public mind. But in the short run of a presidential campaign, people still react to candidates in very traditional ways. To get people to change their minds, the candidate must make his positions clear on the right issues, select the appropriate groups and publicize well his support for their goals, and pick the more favorable aspects of his public record and make them broadly known.

In the backroom, on the stump, in the newspaper, this is the political candidate's best strategy for persuasion. It is also his best strategy for political persuasion in the mystical medium of television.

Pursuit of this strategy would also benefit the electorate. Without question, information about the candidates' policies, commitments, and executive abilities provides voters a far more meaningful basis for choosing between the candidates than trivial televised pictures. Although some critics would argue that this strategy eliminates elections as a time for truly major political change, an election can only serve that function when the public wants it, as happened in 1932. The candidate cannot remold public opinion during the campaign, but he can inform the people how he meets their political needs and wants. And that, by any reckoning, is no small improvement over a campaign of meaningless television imagery.

NOTES

PREFACE

1. Although television's impact on American voters has not been re-searched systematically, two such studies have been undertaken in Great Britain. The results are contained in Jay G. Blumler and Denis McQuail, *Television in Politics* (Chicago: University of Chicago Press, 1969), and Joseph Trenaman and Denis McQuail, *Television and the Political Image* (London: Methuen and Co. Ltd., 1961).

2. Herbert E. Alexander, "Communications and Politics: The Media and the Message," in Robert Agranoff (ed), *The New Style in Election Campaigns* (Boston: Holbrook Press, 1972), pp. 371–2.

3. The research was conducted under National Science Foundation grant GS-35408, "Voting Revisited in the Age of Television: The Study of a Political Campaign Using a New Methodology," Robert D. McClure and Thomas E. Patterson, co-principal investigators.

INTRODUCTION: THE MISTAKEN VIEW OF TELEVISED POLITICS

1. *Voters' Time: Report of the Twentieth Century Fund Commission on Campaign Costs in the Electronic Era* (New York: Twentieth Century Fund, 1969). (Emphasis added.)

2. These various claims about televised politics have been made in innumerable books and articles. See, for example, Robert MacNeil, *The People Machine* (New York: Harper and Row, 1968); Dan Nimmo, *The Political Persuaders* (Englewood Cliffs, N.J.: Prentice-Hall, 1970); Gene Wyckoff, *The Image Candidates* (New York: The Macmillan Company, 1968); Joe

McGinniss, *The Selling of the President 1968* (New York: Trident Press, 1969).

3. Quite literally, the findings and arguments in this book apply only to voters in *presidential general elections*. In short, our claims are confined to our data base, and we make no arguments here about television's influence in Senatorial races, in local mayoral races, or even in presidential primaries.

CHAPTER 1. NETWORK EVENING NEWS COVERAGE OF A PRESIDENTIAL CAMPAIGN

1. NBC evening news, October 3, 1972.

2. CBS evening news, October 9, 1972.

3. The news minutes shown in Table 2 are a generous estimate of network news coverage of the candidates' qualifications. Not only are references from any source included, but a liberal interpretation of what constituted a reference to the candidates' abilities or characters was used. If a strict definition had been used, and only references originating with network anchormen or correspondents included, the news minutes shown would have dwindled to almost nothing for all three networks.

4. See, MacNeil, op. cit.; Nimmo, op. cit.; Wyckoff, op. cit.

5. Kurt Lang and Gladys Engel Lang, *Politics and Television* (Chicago: Quadrangle Books, 1968), chapters 5, 8.

6. MacNeil, op. cit., p. 50.

7. ABC evening news, October 23, 1972.

8. News minutes shown for candidates' personal and leadership qualifications are the sum of news minutes given to the twenty-four candidate traits listed in Table 1 which was presented earlier in this chapter. News minutes shown for candidates' stands on key issues are the sum of news minutes given to the twenty-six issue positions listed in Table 2 which was presented earlier in this chapter. News minutes shown for campaign activity include time given to such things as size and enthusiasm of crowds at the candidates' rallies, motorcade scenes and routes, candidates' standings in public opinion polls, candidates' plans and strategies, labor endorsements, campaign appearances by candidates' wives and children. Table is based only on news stories explicitly about the 1972 election campaign.

9. News stories are those presented on NBC evening news from October 31, 1972, to November 6, 1972 (weekdays only). Stories shown include only those explicitly about the 1972 election campaign.

CHAPTER 2. NETWORK EVENING NEWS AND AN INFORMED ELECTORATE

1. Richard M. Nixon, *The Six Crises* (New York: Doubleday, 1962), p. 422.

2. MacNeil, op. cit., p. 184.

3. Quoted from an article furnished one of the authors by Edwin Diamond.

4. A full explanation of the figures is contained in Appendix D.

5. Quoted in Martin Mayer, *About Television* (New York: Harper and Row, 1972), p. 192.

6. MacNeil, op. cit., p. 40.

7. Leo Bogart, *Strategy in Advertising* (New York: Harcourt, Brace, and World, 1967), p. 139.

8. Herbert E. Krugman, "The Impact of Television Advertising: Learning Without Involvement," *Public Opinion Quarterly*, XXIX (Fall, 1965), pp. 349–365.

9. *Television and Growing Up: The Impact of Televised Violence*, Report of the Surgeon General's Scientific Advisory Committee on Television and Social Behavior (Rockville, Maryland: National Institute of Mental Health, 1971).

10. Responses come from interviews conducted with potential voters during the 1972 general election. Responses have been edited to improve readability. Ages and occupations have been changed to protect identities of respondents.

CHAPTER 3. NETWORK EVENING NEWS AND THE IMAGES OF CANDIDATES

1. Quoted in Rowland Evans, "TV in the Political Campaign," *Television Quarterly*, V (Winter, 1966), p. 25.

2. McGinniss, op. cit., pp. 29–30.

3. Quoted in ibid., pp. 193–4.

4. MacNeil, op. cit.; Nimmo, op. cit.; Wyckoff, op. cit.

5. Marshall McLuhan, *Understanding Media* (New York: McGraw-Hill Book Co., 1964), p. 280.

6. Quoted in MacNeil, op. cit., p. 139.

7. Nimmo, op. cit., p. 144.

8. Ibid.

9. William Sansom, *A Contest of Ladies* (London: Hogarth, 1956), pp. 230–2, cited in Erving Goffman, *The Presentation of Self to Others* (New York: Doubleday, 1959), pp. 3–4.

10. CBS evening news, October 12, 1971.

11. Selective perception of political phenomena has been a frequent research subject, see, e.g., Bernard Berelson, Paul Lazarsfeld, and William McPhee, *Voting* (Chicago: University of Chicago Press, 1954). Its relevance as an explanation for candidates' images, however, has seldom been examined systematically. One instance where it has is Roberta S. Sigel's, "Effect of Partisanship on the Perception of Political Candidates," *Public Opinion Quarterly*, XXVIII (Fall, 1964), pp. 483–96.

12. Multiscopic studies apparently have not been conducted using political objects. Party symbols and candidates' pictures might be suitable objects for multiscopic experiments which could, as an example, be used to measure underlying partisan sentiments.

13. Gordon W. Allport and Leo J. Postman, "The Basic Psychology of Rumor," pp. 54–65 in Eleanor E. Maccoby, et al. (eds), *Readings in Social Psychology* (New York: Holt, Rinehart, and Winston, 1958).

14. Angus Campbell, Phillip Converse, Warren Miller, Donald Stokes, *The American Voter* (New York: John Wiley and Sons, 1964, abridged edition), chapters 5, 7, 11–15.

15. Jacques Ellul, *Propaganda* (New York: Alfred A. Knopf, 1964), pp. 18–19; Harold Mendelsohn and Irving Crespi, *Polls, Television, and the New Politics* (Scranton, Pa.: Chandler Publishing Co., 1970), pp. 251–3.

16. Responses come from interviews conducted with potential voters during the 1972 general election. Responses have been edited to improve readability. Ages and occupations have been changed to protect identities of respondents.

17. Previous studies have amply demonstrated that those voters who decide earlier in the campaign how they will vote are more attentive and informed than late deciders. See, e.g., Berelson, et al., op. cit., p. 20.

18. Most undecided voters have little systematic change in their images prior to choosing a candidate. Up to that point, their images are relatively stable and do not strongly favor either candidate. After they select a candidate, however, their images change dramatically and systematically. They develop a better image of the candidate they selected and a worse image of his opponent.

19. The television theory of images contends that television communicates distinct images—favorable or unfavorable. For the theory to be correct, a candidate's image must be uniform for television viewers. McGovern's image obviously was not uniform, but good or bad depending on people's political leanings. The only plausible conclusion is that television does not project unique images.

20. People's political orientations were determined from their preferences on eleven issues and where they thought Nixon and McGovern stood on these issues. If their issue preferences were clearly more compatible with Nixon's, they were classified as con-McGovern. If their issue preferences were clearly more aligned with McGovern's, they were classified as pro-McGovern. If their issue preferences fell between the candidates, they were classified as neutral-McGovern.

21. This conclusion is consistent with V. O. Key's thesis about voters. See, V. O. Key, Jr., *The Responsible Electorate* (Cambridge, Mass.: The Belknap Press, 1966).

CHAPTER 4. NETWORK EVENING NEWS AND THE PUBLIC AGENDA

1. Theodore White, *The Making of the President 1972* (New York: Bantam, 1973), p. 327.

2. Bernard Cohen, *The Press, the Public and Foreign Policy* (Princeton, N.J.: Princeton University Press, 1963), p. 13.

3. The agenda-setting power of the press recently has been an object of research interest to communication scholars. These scholars particularly have been interested in the press' ability to create in people's minds a sense of importance about the public issues it emphasizes. See, e.g., Maxwell E. McCombs and Donald L. Shaw, "The Agenda-Setting Function of the Mass Media," *Public Opinion Quarterly*, XXXVI (Summer, 1972), pp. 176–187.

4. Walter Lippmann, *Public Opinion* (New York: The Macmillan Company, 1922), chapter 1.

5. Ibid, p. 29.

6. See, e.g., McCombs and Shaw, op. cit.

7. See, Ithiel de Sola Pool, Robert P. Abelson, and Samuel L. Popkin, *Candidates, Issues, and Strategies* (Cambridge, Mass.: The M.I.T. Press, 1965).

8. Harvey K. Jacobsen, "Mass Media Believability: A Study of Receiver Judgments," *Journalism Quarterly*, XLVI (Spring, 1969), pp. 20–28; Richard F. Carter and Bradley S. Greenberg, "Newspapers or Television: Which Do You Believe?", *Journalism Quarterly*, XLII (Winter, 1965), pp. 29–34; Burns W. Roper, "A Ten-Year View of Public Attitudes Toward Television and Other Mass Media 1959–1968," Television Information Office, New York, 1969.

9. Responses come from interviews conducted with potential voters during the 1972 general election. Responses have been edited to improve

readability. Ages and occupations have been changed to protect identities of respondents.

10. Ralph L. Lowenstein, "Why Network TV News Is Criticized," Freedom of Information Center Report No. 0012, School of Journalism, University of Missouri at Columbia, May, 1971, p. 2, quoted in Wamsley and Pride, op. cit., p. 440.

11. Highly informed and attentive people may see the political significance of events without much help from the mass media, but most people rely on the media for the interpretation of events, particularly those events without direct impact on their daily lives.

12. The emerging corruption issue was the other major news story of the campaign, but at this point there was a great deal of uncertainty about Watergate. Even when this uncertainty is acknowledged, however, network reporting on corrupt activities certainly was no exception to the general pattern of superficial news coverage. Watergate was a complicated chain of events. During the campaign, the facts were uncertain and confusing. The allegations were numerous and varied greatly in their believability. The persons involved were many, sometimes obscure, and frequently only indirectly linked to high officials in the Nixon Administration. Despite the complex nature of the story, however, the networks, excepting CBS, did not attempt to put the pieces together for the viewers. CBS did present two lengthy Watergate reports during the closing days of the 1972 campaign and its reports on the corruption issue averaged 149 seconds. The two lengthy CBS stories consisted of a 15-minute report, delivered on October 27, about the Watergate break-in and where responsibility for it appeared to rest, and an 8-minute report, delivered on October 31, about the financing behind Watergate. But ABC's reports on the corruption issue averaged only 92 seconds and NBC's reports lasted only 57 seconds on the average.

13. Using seven-point scales similar to those described in Appendix D, the same respondents were asked to indicate the personal importance they attached to the Vietnam issue both early in the general election campaign and just prior to election day. Since the same people were questioned on both occasions, it was possible to determine whether the issue became more important to regular news viewers than to nonregular viewers.

14. Quoted from a working paper provided one of the authors by Av Westin of ABC News.

15. Ibid.; Small, op. cit.

16. Edward Jay Epstein, *News From Nowhere* (New York: Random House, 1973), p. 152.

17. At a research conference held in Chicago in December, 1974, Professor Doris Graber of the University of Illinois at Chicago Circle indicated that the pictures of a network news story communicate a message quite different from the audio message about thirty percent of the time.

18. Table based on people's replies to the question: "What one thing that you saw on television stands out most in your mind?" An example of a video-dominated response is, "I saw McGovern shaking hands with people." An example of an audio-dominated response is, "George McGovern said he wanted to reduce military spending."

19. Responses come from interviews conducted with potential voters during the 1972 general election. Responses have been edited to improve readability. Ages and occupations have been changed to protect identities of respondents.

CHAPTER 5. PACKAGING PRESIDENTIAL CANDIDATES: TELEVISED POLITICAL COMMERCIALS

1. See, e.g., MacNeil, op. cit., chapter 8; Arthur Schlesinger, Jr., *TV Guide,* October 22, 1966, p. 9.

2. Quoted in Martin Mayer, op. cit., p. 247.

3. See, e.g., MacNeil, op. cit.; Wyckoff, op. cit.; Nimmo, op. cit.

4. Ibid.

5. Interview conducted by authors with William Taylor, creator of televised commercials for the 1972 Nixon campaign.

6. Bogart, op. cit.

7. McGinniss, op. cit., p. 38.

8. Classification based on dominant emphasis of the televised spots used by Nixon and McGovern. Few spots, however, are either pure issue or pure image commercials. Most ads combine issue and image appeals.

CHAPTER 6. THE IMPACT OF TELEVISED POLITICAL COMMERCIALS

1. Tom Wicker, "TV in the Political Campaign," *Television Quarterly,* IV (Spring, 1965), p. 14.

2. Samuel L. Becker and Elmer W. Lower, "Broadcasting in Presidential Campaigns," in Sidney Kraus (ed.), *Great Debates* (Bloomington: Indiana University Press, 1962), p. 50, cited in MacNeil, op. cit., p. 196.

3. Bogart, op. cit., p. 139.

4. Respondents were first asked whether they had seen a Nixon or McGovern commercial. If they indicated seeing an ad, they were then asked: "Would you tell me what you can about the Nixon (McGovern)

commercial you remember best?" Those remembering nothing about the ad were classified as "unable to recall." Other replies were classified as partial or full recall depending on whether respondents stated the central message of the commercial they had seen.

5. Bogart, op. cit., p. 139.

6. Raymond A. Bauer and Stephen A. Greyser, *Advertising in America* (Boston: Harvard University Press, 1968), chapter 7.

7. Ibid. Percentages based on a reconstruction of data contained in source.

8. In elections below the office of the presidency, televised advertising may have some impact on voters' images of the candidates. First, voters are less involved in these elections and their defense mechanisms against political propaganda are not as fully activated. Consequently, advertising imagery does not encounter such intense resistance as in presidential campaigns. Second, voters are less likely to have information about the candidates' policies and public records in lower-level elections. For many voters, their total knowledge of the candidates will not exceed name awareness and party affiliation. Undoubtedly, party affiliation is the major influence on voters' images of these candidates but, at the same time, advertising may play some role because it is not overwhelmed by other influences. For many of these same reasons, and because party identification loses its significance, primary elections may also be more fertile grounds for successful advertising imagery.

9. People's political orientations were determined from the proximity of their preferences on eleven issues to the positions they felt the candidates held on the same issues. Those respondents whose issue stands more closely matched Nixon's were classified as pro-Nixon and those whose preferences more closely matched McGovern's were classified as pro-McGovern. Respondents whose issue preferences fell about equally between the candidates' positions are not included in the table.

10. Responses come from interviews conducted with potential voters during the 1972 general election. Responses have been edited to improve readability. Ages and occupations have been changed to protect identities of respondents.

11. The data reveal a slightly better image for McGovern among people who remained undecided throughout the campaign. Advertising clearly was not the reason, since his image was slightly better among people with both light and heavy advertising exposure. Most of these respondents were disinterested citizens with Democratic leanings and, likely, their partisan sentiments explain their evaluations of McGovern.

12. Image change for undecided voters, regardless of their advertising exposure, fit a random pattern prior to their selecting a candidate. *After they had made their choice,* their images altered substantially. The image of

their chosen candidate improved dramatically and the image of their rejected candidate became worse.

13. Responses come from interviews conducted with potential voters during the 1972 general election. Responses have been edited to improve readability. Ages and occupations have been changed to protect identities of respondents.

14. Responses come from interviews conducted with potential voters during the 1972 general election. Responses have been edited to improve readability. Ages and occupations have been changed to protect identities of respondents.

15. See, e.g., *Voters' Time: Report of the Twentieth Century Fund Commission on Campaign Costs in the Electronic Era*, op. cit.

16. Ibid., p. 2.

17. Data are is based on respondents' reported viewing of nine 30-minute television broadcasts sponsored by Nixon and McGovern during the 1972 general election.

18. Lippmann, op. cit., Chapter 23.

CHAPTER 7.   DO POLITICAL COMMERCIALS MANIPULATE THE UNINFORMED VOTER?

1. MacNeil, op. cit., p. 224.

2. Nimmo, op. cit., p. 118.

3. Previous research has repeatedly demonstrated that media usage is heavily stratified. Those people who follow the campaign in one news medium are more likely to follow it in others; people who avoid the campaign in a news medium are more likely to avoid it in other mediums. See, Berelson, et al., op. cit., chapter 11; Paul Lazarsfeld, Bernard Berelson, and Hazel Gaudet, *The People's Choice* (New York: The Columbia University Press, 1948), chapter 14.

4. See, for example, discussion contained in Berelson, et al., op. cit., chapter 14; Campbell, et al., op. cit., chapter 17.

5. MacNeil, op. cit., pp. 3–4; Nimmo, op. cit., pp. 114–117. Data from the survey on which this book is based indicate that regular viewers of television entertainment programs have, compared with the total population, almost identical education levels, incomes, and news media exposure levels.

6. See, e.g., Berelson, et al., op. cit.; Campbell, et al., op. cit.; Lazarsfeld, et al., op. cit.

7. Ibid. Research conducted over the past three decades indicates that the vast majority of America's highly informed voters make their vote choice prior to the general election campaign and neither waver from nor change that choice during the campaign.

8. Responses come from interviews conducted with potential voters during the 1972 general election. Responses have been edited to improve readability. Ages and occupations have been changed to protect identities of respondents.

CHAPTER 8. RESPONSIBLE JOURNALISM AND RATIONAL CANDIDATES

1. Timothy Crouse, *The Boys on the Bus* (New York: Ballantine Books, 1972), p. 154.

2. Key, op. cit., pp. 6–8.

3. MacNeil, op. cit., p. 14.

4. Ibid., pp. 28–9.

5. Ibid., p. 50.

6. Ibid., p. 36.

7. Epstein, op. cit., pp. 91–6.

8. These recommendations follow from those made by MacNeil, op. cit., pp. 50–1.

9. Three special election issue reports were presented on the CBS Evening News during the 1972 campaign's final days. The first, presented on October 30, contrasted Nixon's and McGovern's positions on military defense. It was more than six minutes in length. On November 2, a report on the candidates' economic issue positions was broadcast and it lasted about four minutes. The final report, covering a range of issues and lasting over six minutes, was carried on November 6. Graphics, existing film, and Walter Cronkite's communication skills combined to make these issue reports both informative and visually interesting.

10. Responses come from interviews conducted with potential voters during the 1972 general election. Responses have been edited to improve readability. Ages and occupations have been changed to protect identities of respondents.

11. See the communication research findings discussed in Joseph T. Klapper, *The Effects of Mass Communication* (New York: The Free Press, 1960).

12. See, e.g., Richard W. Boyd, "Popular Control of Public Policy: A Normal Vote Analysis of the 1968 Election," *American Political Science Review* 66 (1972), pp. 429–449; Richard A. Brody and Benjamin I. Page,

"Comment: The Assessment of Policy Voting," *American Political Science Review* 66 (1972), pp. 450–458; Philip E. Converse, et al., "Continuity and Change in American Politics: Parties and Issues in the 1968 Election," *American Political Science Review* 63 (1969), pp. 1083–1105; Martin Fishbein and Fred Coombs, "Basis for Decision: An Attitudinal Approach Toward an Understanding of Voting Behavior," paper presented at the 67th Annual Meeting of the American Political Science Association, Chicago, September 7–11, 1971; John H. Kessel, "Comment: The Issues in Issue Voting," *American Political Science Review* 66 (1972), pp. 459–465; V. O. Key, Jr., op. cit.; Norman H. Nie, "Mass Belief Systems Revisited: Political Change and Attitude Structure," unpublished paper, University of Chicago, 1972; Gerald M. Pomper, "From Confusion to Clarity: Issues and American Voters, 1956–1968," *American Political Science Review* 66 (1972), pp. 415–428; David E. Repass, "Issue Salience and Party Choice," *American Political Science Review* 65 (1971), pp. 389–400; Michael J. Shapiro, "Rational Political Man: A Synthesis of Economic and Socio-Psychological Perspectives," *American Political Science Review* 60 (1966), pp. 19–28.

13. Key, op. cit., p. 9.

14. For a more complete development of this argument, see Nimmo, op. cit., Chapter 5.

APPENDIX A

The Survey and the Questionnaire

TO estimate the media's election impact, *panel* survey data was collected. In a panel survey, the key factor is that the *same* individuals are interviewed on several occasions. For this study respondents were interviewed in early September, early October, early November (just before Election Day), and mid-November (just after Election Day). Since many of the *same* questions were asked during each interview, people's answers from one interview to the next provided an accurate indicator of changes in their thinking over the course of the campaign. To estimate the part the mass media played in this process, the changes in people's thinking were related to what they saw, heard, and read during the campaign.

The value of a panel survey becomes apparent when it is compared with what is called a *cross-sectional* survey. A cross-sectional survey involves a *single* interview with people. If the media's influence is to be assessed using this technique, people are required to *recall* how they felt. Such recall is greatly affected by memory loss, imprecision, and rationalization. Also many people are not conscious of gradual changes in their thinking. Most people, for example, would not have been aware that their images of presidential candidates systematically adjusted during the general election campaign.

There is another problem with cross-sectional data—what people think at any given time is the result of many factors. Many of the opinions and much of the political knowledge that people possess are acquired early in life and reflect the influence of factors other than the media, such as people's education, occupational situation, and family influences. Using cross-sectional data, it is a nightmarish task to determine how much of what people know and think is attributable to their media exposure during the campaign and how much is attributable to these other factors.

With panel data the problem is less imposing. The initial interview provides a baseline measure of what people know and what they think. Subsequent interviews then provide a more precise basis for determining what changes occurred during the interview period. Knowing these specific changes and the precise time they occurred increases the likelihood of isolating the media's campaign effects.

Past research justifies the need for a panel survey. Some scholars have tried to assess media effects using cross-sectional survey data, but theirs has been a thankless, and often foolhardy, task. Those studies which have successfully isolated campaign effects, from the Lazarsfeld and Berelson studies of the 1940's to the more recent Blumler-McQuail study in Great Britain, have employed panel designs.

The panel survey used in this research involved three personal interviews, each over an hour in length, conducted before Election Day, and one brief postelection telephone interview. The typical respondent submitted to almost four hours of interviewing during the 1972 general election. Since the total length of the combined questionnaires exceeds one hundred pages, the survey questions cannot be completely duplicated here. Provided below, however, is a partial listing of information gathered during the interviews.

	Interview(s) During Which Information Was Obtained			
	1st	2nd	3rd	4th
1. Recall of, and reaction to, recent network news reports	X	X	X	
2. Recall of, and reaction to,	X	X	X	

	1st	2nd	3rd	4th
recent newspaper stories				
3. Recall of, and reaction to, political commercials		X	X	
4. Network evening news viewing frequency	X	X	X	
5. Newspaper reading frequency	X	X	X	
6. Television programming viewing frequency	X	X	X	
7. Radio listening frequency		X		
8. Magazine reading frequency		X		
9. Political conversation frequency	X	X	X	
10. Exposure to half-hour televised political broadcasts		X	X	X
11. Exposure to newspaper political advertising		X		
12. Exposure to radio political advertising		X	X	
13. Respondent ranking of importance of various information sources	X	X	X	
14. Respondent ranking of importance of various influence sources	X	X	X	
15. Trust in various media sources			X	
16. Perceptions of bias in media sources			X	
17. Recall of, and reaction to, personal conversations about campaign	X	X	X	
18. Respondent judgment about most important quality for a President to have	X		X	
19. Respondent judgment about the most important political problem	X	X	X	
20. Respondent party identification	X		X	
21. Respondent ideology	X		X	

	1st	2nd	3rd	4th
22. Organizations to which respondent pays attention when it comes to politics	X		X	
23. People to whom respondent pays attention when it comes to politics	X		X	
24. Reaction to party conventions and party nominees	X			
25. Voting intentions of friends, family and co-workers	X		X	
26. Letters received from candidate organizations/political parties	X	X	X	
27. Telephone calls received from candidate organizations/ political parties	X	X	X	
28. Literature received from candidate organizations/ political parties	X	X	X	
29. Personal contacts made by candidate organizations/ political parties	X	X	X	
30. Voting intention	X	X	X	X
31. Turnout intention	X	X	X	X
32. Reasons for change (if any) in vote intention		X	X	X
33. Reasons for change (if any) in turnout intention		X	X	X
34. Respondent knowledge of details of election issues	X	X	X	
35. Respondent awareness of candidates' issue stands (see Appendix D)	X	X	X	
36. Respondent beliefs about the candidates' images (see Appendix D)	X	X	X	
37. Respondent judgments about the salience of issues/ image traits	X	X	X	
38. Respondent judgments about	X	X	X	

	1st	2nd	3rd	4th
the salience of issues to the candidates				
39. Respondent interest in politics (9 items)		X		
40. Respondent beliefs about political parties (12 items)		X		
41. Respondent knowledge of candidate appearances in area	X		X	
42. Demographic data on respondent	X			
43. Respondent satisfaction with personal economic situation	X			
44. Respondent motivations for following campaign		X		
45. Respondent motivations for avoiding campaign		X		
46. Respondent ticket-splitting behavior		X		X
47. Respondent voting history		X		
48. Respondent family background relating to politics		X		
49. Respondent judgments about good and bad points of Nixon and McGovern		X		
50. Respondent judgments about completeness of coverage provided by various news media		X		
51. Respondent judgments about impartiality of coverage provided by various news media		X		
52. Respondent judgments about enjoyability of coverage provided by various news sources		X		
53. Respondent preferences for television news election coverage		X		
54. Respondent activity (e.g., financial contributions) in campaign			X	

	1st	2nd	3rd	4th
55. Respondent efforts at interpersonal political influence			X	
56. Respondent membership in organizations			X	
57. Respondent attitudes toward various groups			X	
58. Respondent attention to various sections of the newspaper			X	
59. Respondent reaction to the way Nixon and McGovern ran their campaigns			X	
60. Frequency with which respondent talked politics with others		X	X	
61. Frequency with which respondent listened to news on radio		X	X	

APPENDIX B

The Fieldwork and Sample

A total of 2,707 interviews were conducted with eligible voters during the 1972 general election: 731 respondents were interviewed in the early September wave, 650 of these 731 respondents were interviewed again in early October, 650 of the initial 731 were interviewed again in early November (just before Election Day). These three preelection interviews were personal interviews. In addition, 676 of the original 731 respondents were contacted for a brief, postelection, telephone interview.

The field work was carried out by a team of paid, and mostly professional, interviewers who were recruited through referral by a professional survey supervisor and by public advertisement. About seventy-five percent of the interviewers had substantial experience in either market or public opinion interviewing. A lengthy training session was held before the first interview and a thorough briefing session was conducted before the remaining interviews. In addition, each interviewer conducted at least two sample interviews before the first wave, and one before the second and third waves. Fieldwork was supervised by the authors and their research coordinator, Richard Ender. In addition, three research assistants and four graduate students assisted with in-house activity. A pretest of the questionnaire was conducted through about thirty pilot interviews. Certain portions of the interview schedule were then altered and pretests were conducted on approximately forty more pilot respondents.

The sample was drawn from a medium-size metropolitan area. As defined by the United States Bureau of the Census, the research site is in the midrange of the nation's 100 largest metropolitan areas. Several considerations prompted this selection. First, the metropolitan area has television stations affiliated with each of the national networks—ABC, CBS, and NBC. Thus, the nightly newscasts of all three networks were available to the population, as well as advertising time purchased by the candidates on any of the networks. Second, the area has both a morning and an evening newspaper that contain about as much news content as the average daily newspaper in the nation. Third, the site was proximate to the available research resources. Fourth, the site is considered a "typical" American metropolitan area. Because of this, it is a frequently used site for market research. Also, most national survey organizations, such as Gallup and the Survey Research Center, use the area as a sampling point. These features of the area insured the availability of competent interviewers.

Since the site is considered typical, confidence in the wider applicability of the research findings is increased. The decision to use a single area sample, rather than a national sample, is consistent with most academic and market surveys designed to test the effects of the mass media. The noted campaign studies conducted by Paul Lazarsfeld and Bernard Berelson in the nineteen-forties, for example, were done in single locations. The major advantage of a single location sample is that it holds constant other environmental influences operating on individuals, which increases the research's internal validity. Internal validity—the assurance that the media are, or are not, the major explanatory factor accounting for observed voter change—is crucial. Without this assurance, no significance can be attached to the findings. However, the research does raise the question of external validity, or the finding's applicability to the broader American electorate. Some concern must persist, but several reasons suggest that the research findings broadly apply. First, the research is concerned with a stimulus common to the broader electorate. If the study examined the campaign effects of political party canvassing, which varies widely from area to area, the results would be hard to generalize. But network television campaign communication, whether on the news or through advertising, varies only minimally across the country. Second, the research is limited to effects for which local variation is likely to be unimportant. For instance, neither people's issue information nor their media use varies widely between locations and it is reasonable to assume that what voters in one area learn or fail to learn from television is paralleled in other locations. Third, media relationships were, whenever it seemed relevant, controlled for variables which might affect those relationships and which do vary from location to location. People's political orientations, for example, were held constant in examining media impact on images. Thus, although these orientations are not evenly distributed throughout the country, controlling for them allows their effect to be partialled out in the analysis. Fourth, the findings make sense. For example, television news contains little issue information and people learn almost nothing about the issues from watching it; television advertising says something about the candidates' issue positions and voters do learn where the candidates stand from watching it.

The sample was a stratified random sample. The sample was stratified to increase variation in partisan loyalty. The sample was drawn using 200 blocks obtained through the skip interval technique using data from the 1970 United States Census. This included one empty block which was discarded. Field examination of each block was carried out to designate randomly a sample cluster of seven households in each of which one adult over eighteen years of age was randomly selected through a respondent selection grid.

The first wave of interviews was held between September 7 and 18. This resulted in 731 individuals being successfully interviewed, which is 52 percent of the sample drawn and 56 percent adjusted to eliminate ineligible respondents. Details of the nonparticipants in the first wave are described in Table 1.

The results of the second wave of interviewing are contained in Table 2. Conducted between October 7 and 15, the 650 completed interviews amounted to 89 percent of the reduced sample. In addition, 20 respondents who could not be contacted in person during the period were interviewed by telephone for key portions of the interviews.

TABLE 1. Nonparticipants in Precampaign—Wave 1

	N	%
Eligible:		
Refusal	270	40
Not home, not contacted	260	39
subtotal		79
Disqualified:		
Too infirm or ill	28	4
Could not read and/or speak English	11	2
Not U.S. Citizen	17	3
Moving before completion of survey	17	3
Address vacant or demolished	23	3
Other disqualifications	2	–
subtotal		15
Reasons not ascertained	41	6
Total	669	100

TABLE 2. Interviewing Results in Midcampaign—Wave 2

Eligible Respondents	N	%
Successfully interviewed	650	89
Not contacted in field, but interviewed by telephone	20	3
Refusal	39	5
Not home, not contacted	18	2
Illness	2	–
Moved, with no forwarding address	2	–
Total	731	100

The third wave was conducted between October 30 and November 6. The results are shown in Table 3 and, again, 650 of the original respondents were contacted.

TABLE 3. Interviewing Results at Campaign End—Wave 3

Eligible Respondents	N	%
Successfully interviewed	650	89
Refusal	26	4
Not home, not contacted	8	1
Illness	1	–
Moved, with no forwarding address	1	–
Not contacted for Wave 3	45	6
Total	731	100

Overall, 626—or 86 percent—of the original panel were interviewed all three times prior to the election. This retention rate is extremely high (by way of comparison, the rate for the three personal interviews of the well-known Elmira study was 72 percent). In addition to the three preelection personal interviews, a short postelection telephone interview was conducted. Of the 731 original respondents, 676 were contacted for this final interview—a 92 percent completion rate.

As an incentive for participation, respondents were told after completion of the first wave that they would receive $2 as a token payment for each completed personal interview. The money was sent to respondents along with a thank-you letter and the next announcement that the interviewer would soon be calling on them again.

Panel representativeness is shown in Table 4 on five selected demographic indicators. Females and low- and high-income individuals were slightly oversampled, while young voters were slightly undersampled. None of these differences, however, significantly alter the overall representativeness of the sample.

TABLE 4. Comparative Information on Representativeness of Final Panel Sample

	Panel Distribution	Real Urbanized Distribution
Sex:		
Male	43%	48%
Female	57	52
Race:		
White	92	93
Nonwhite	8	7
City/Suburbs:		
City	54	52
County	46	48
Income:		
Under $5,999	24*	20
$ 6,000–$9,999	20	26
$10,000–$14,999	26	30
$15,000 and over	30	23
Age:		
18 to 24	13*	19
25 to 34	22	18
35 to 44	18	17
45 to 54	19	18
55 to 64	14	13
over 65	14	14

*Income and age reported by respondent

APPENDIX C

Measuring Media Content

CAMPAIGN television was monitored for the period September 18 through November 6, 1972. During that period, every weeknight evening newscast of ABC, CBS, and NBC was viewed and recorded. Also during that time, every televised political commercial shown by Nixon and McGovern was viewed and recorded. This material provided the raw data for the media content analysis presented in this book.

Television News Content

Two research assistants were assigned to watch the evening news newscasts of each network. While watching, they were instructed to provide certain information about the visual content of the news. They had as their primary responsibilities to indicate (1) the method by which each news report was presented (e.g., face-to-camera reporting, slides, film), (2) the method by which candidates were presented (e.g., slides, film, quoted by newsmen, mentioned in a news story), and (3) the settings in which candidates were presented (e.g., alone, with another person, in a small group, at a meeting, in a large crowd). Additionally, these research assistants wrote down their impressions of the completeness, artificiality, and distortion of each news report. This material guided the authors in their judgments about the nature of television reporting.

The research assistants also recorded on audio tape the

weeknight evening newscasts of the three networks. After the election, these tapes were content analyzed by a staff of paid coders who underwent a one-week training session prior to beginning their task. The newscasts were coded on a story-by-story basis. The following guidelines were followed in determining what would be considered a "story." Whenever topic and reporting source changed at the same time, a "story" was defined as beginning. Assume, for example, that a correspondent was delivering a report on the Middle East and, upon its completion, the anchorman came on camera and reported the results of the latest Gallup Poll on the presidential race. The poll report was considered a discrete story. Except in one situation, a change in reporting source, even when the topic stayed the same, was also considered to signal the start of a new story. Assume, for example, that one correspondent delivered a report of a Washington *Post* story on Watergate and, immediately thereafter, another correspondent conducted a filmed interview with Jerome Barkun about Watergate, but not about the *Post* story. The Barkun interview was considered a discrete story although, like the *Post* report, it fell under the general topic of Watergate. The only time that a shift in reporting source was not considered to signal another story was when the anchorman supplied a lead-in or concluding comment to a correspondent's report.

Not all news stories shown on the evening news were content analyzed. Only those stories directly about the campaign (e.g., a report of a candidate appearing at an election rally) or clearly relevant to the campaign (e.g., a report on the Paris peace talks) were coded. Using this criteria of inclusion, 251 of ABC's stories, 249 of CBS's, and 238 of NBC's were content analyzed. Table 1 contains a list of these stories by network and topic. They accounted for over forty percent of all news stories carried on the networks' weeknight newscasts during the period of analysis. The remaining sixty percent of news stories which were not analyzed covered such subjects as airplane crashes and other disasters, human interest stories, reports on foreign developments that seemed remote

TABLE 1. Network Coverage of Various Events and Public
Problems (September 18–November 6, 1972)

Event or Public Problem	Number of Stories		
	ABC	CBS	NBC
Presidential campaign	143	147	122
Vietnam:			
Peace efforts	35	33	42
Administration's handling of war	2	2	1
Vietnam withdrawal	3	1	1
Prisoners of war	0	0	1
Corruption:			
Watergate incident	18	26	26
Russian wheat deal	7	8	5
Corruption (general)	6	4	8
Other:			
Level of government spending	6	3	5
Relations with U.S.S.R.	3	5	6
Inflation, cost of living	4	3	4
Busing	3	2	1
Economic situation (general)	1	1	2
Unemployment	2	2	1
Taxes	0	0	2
Veterans	1	0	2
Welfare	1	3	1
All others (no more than one mention on a network)	16	9	8
TOTALS	251	249	238

from the 1972 election (e.g., strife in Ireland), daily stock
market reports, routine reports on Vietnam combat action
and weekly casualty statistics (unless some comment was
made on their relevance to the election), stories on sporting
events (such as the World Series), etc.

In analyzing those news stories which were of interest,
most of the categories used in the analysis need no explanation: total story length, time given to film, candidate-on-cam-

era time, correspondent who delivered the report, major topic of the report.

The most critical code in the analysis, however, requires some explanation. This code was designed to capture what was said about a candidate, who said it, and how clear the reference was. This code provided the basis for determining the amount of time that the networks awarded to coverage of specific issue stands taken by the candidates and the specific personal and leadership traits possessed by them. This material, of course, was the basis for the conclusions in Chapter One about network news' coverage of election issues and candidate character.

This material was obtained in the following manner. First, code categories were established for the candidate policy stands and the personal/leadership candidate traits that seemed important in the 1972 election. Some twenty-six policies (fifteen for Nixon and eleven for McGovern) were selected for inclusion:

Relations with China (Nixon)
Relations with Soviet Union (Nixon)
Handling of Vietnam War (Nixon)
Immediate withdrawal from Vietnam (McGovern)
Amnesty for draft evaders (Nixon/McGovern)
Taxes on people with high incomes (Nixon/ McGovern)
Drug abuse (Nixon/McGovern)
Law and order (Nixon/McGovern)
Military spending level (Nixon/McGovern)
Government spending level (Nixon)
Honoring commitments to other nations (Nixon/ McGovern)
Government guaranteed jobs for unemployed (McGovern)
Handling of unemployment (Nixon)
Making people on welfare go to work (Nixon/McGovern)
Busing (Nixon/McGovern)
Wiping out political corruption and favoritism (Nixon/ McGovern)
Handling of inflation (Nixon)

And some twenty-four personal and leadership traits were selected for inclusion (twelve for each candidate):

Experience in government (Nixon/McGovern)
Personal appealingness (Nixon/McGovern)
Personal trustworthiness (Nixon/McGovern)
Extremism of his politics (Nixon/McGovern)
Understanding of common person (Nixon/McGovern)
Clarity of his political intentions (Nixon/McGovern)
Confidence-inspiring nature of his leadership (Nixon/McGovern)
Forward-looking nature of his leadership (Nixon/McGovern)
Tendency to "play politics" (Nixon/McGovern)
Ability to maintain control over situations (Nixon/McGovern)
Compassion for less fortunate (Nixon/McGovern)
Follows his convictions (Nixon/McGovern)

Using these predetermined categories, the coders were instructed to note each reference to any of the fifty items, to indicate how many news seconds were devoted to each mention, to record the source of the reference, and to judge the clarity of the reference. The following news report will illustrate how this was done:

VIDEO	AUDIO
Motorcade moving through crowded streets Crowd cheering President	REPORTER: The Nixon campaign rolled through the wealthy northern suburbs of New York City, attacking Congress which of course was not there, and warmly embracing the crowds which were on hand. *In a written statement issued on arrival in Westchester county, the Republican candidate contended "the time has come to stand up to the big spenders in Congress." He promised to use every weapon to hold down federal spending.* The economy, though, wasn't as much a

VIDEO	AUDIO
McGovern supporters and protestors picketing Nixon's appearance	focus of protest as the bombing and Vietnam war, especially among small pockets of pro-McGovern supporters along the way. The fifty-mile motorcade route wound through eleven small cities in the
Motorcade winding its way through countryside	solid Republican county which Nixon carried by 28,000 votes in 1968. With the Veterans Day holiday, schools out, and the route directed through the heart of business
Motorcade moving through business district	ness districts, the crowds were standing deep at the curbs and, at times, raced dangerously in and out among five photo trucks and seven press buses packed with
People racing in and out of moving buses	newsmen trying to observe the action of the most extended day of Nixon campaigning thus far. At a couple of points the President's limousine stopped, and as
The Nixons shaking hands with crowd	he worked one side of the crowd, Mrs. Nixon worked the other.

This news story contained a reference to one of the twenty-six election issues which were coded. The reference began with "In a written statement . . ." and ended with ". . . to hold down federal spending." A coder would have recorded the following information: Nixon (the source of the issue reference) said that Nixon (the candidate in the issue reference) favored a reduction (the candidate's position on the issue) in government spending (the issue) in a 12-second (the amount of news time given to the issue reference) network news report.

Once all of the news stories were coded in this manner, a computer program was used to determine the amount of time and number of mentions that network news devoted to each of the twenty-six election issues and twenty-four candidate traits. All *explicit* references to each of the items were summed by network for those news reports that were *directly* about the campaign. As an illustration, Table 2 contains the

TABLE 2. Network News Coverage of Various Issue Stands/Policies of Richard Nixon and George McGovern (September 18–November 6, 1972)

	ABC		CBS		NBC	
	Total News minutes	Number of times mentioned	Total news minutes	Number of times mentioned	Total news minutes	Number of times mentioned
Nixon policies:						
Russia	0:00	0	0:32	3	0:09	1
China	0:00	0	0:36	3	0:00	0
Military spending	1:47	2	1:58	4	0:23	1
Foreign commitments	0:04	1	0:00	0	0:00	0
Busing	0:17	2	1:27	3	0:25	2
Law and order	0:39	1	5:27	7	0:13	1
Taxes on upper-incomes	0:00	0	0:19	2	0:07	1
Government spending	1:32	2	0:30	2	0:47	3
Amnesty	0:00	0	0:03	1	0:00	0
Unemployment	0:05	1	1:14	4	0:35	3
Inflation	0:05	1	0:23	2	0:05	1
Vietnam war	17:57	29	12:26	22	9:10	13
Political corruption	3:58	5	4:02	7	5:42	7
Welfare	0:00	0	0:13	1	0:00	0
Drugs	3:19	5	4:32	6	2:57	5
Totals	29:43	49	33:42	67	20:33	38

McGovern policies:

Taxes on upper-incomes	0	0:00	2	1:01	1	0:06
Jobs for unemployed	0	0:00	2	0:49	1	1:06
Political corruption	2	0:29	2	0:44	1	0:25
Amnesty	0	0:00	2	0:17	0	0:00
Military spending	2	1:45	8	4:50	5	2:10
Vietnam withdrawal	7	1:41	8	3:01	4	1:07
Foreign commitments	2	0:30	2	0:33	1	0:31
Welfare	0	0:00	1	0:25	2	0:09
Law and order	0	0:00	1	0:25	0	0:00
Busing	1	0:07	1	0:13	1	0:07
Drugs	2	1:03	1	0:20	0	0:00
Totals	16	5:35	30	12:38	16	5:41

NOTE: Data include all *explicit* references to the candidates' issue/stands regardless of source in all weeknight network news stories *directly* about the campaign for the period of September 18-November 6, 1972.

amount of news time and number of references, network-by-network, given the twenty-six candidate issue positions. The totals shown in Table 2 are the ones which appeared in Table 3 of Chapter One. Similarly, the totals for the twenty-four candidate traits were shown in Table 2 of Chapter One.

Network news time devoted to campaign activity was also determined through a close story-by-story analysis. Coders were first instructed what was to be considered as campaign activity, e.g., crowd activity, motorcade coverage, reports on hecklers, references to the candidates' strategies, coverage of fund-raising, poll results. Then, they were instructed to record each mention of, and the news seconds awarded to, any campaign activity. The data in Chapter One which shows the total news minutes awarded by each network to campaign activity come from this analysis.

Televised Advertising Content

The information necessary to content analyze the candidates' televised political advertising was obtained through the cooperation of Charles Guggenheim, who produced McGovern's advertising, and William Taylor, who produced Nixon's. They permitted the authors to view and record all of the political spots used during the 1972 general election and furnished logs showing when, through both the networks and television affiliates, the various commercials were shown.

The content analysis of the political ads was similar to the analysis of network news. Each commercial's references to the candidates' issue stands and personal and leadership traits were coded. Then, since some commercials were broadcast several times, these references were multiplied by the number of times the ad in which they appeared was shown during prime-time hours. This provided the total number of mentions and total advertising seconds awarded to each of the twenty-six issue stands and twenty-four personal and leadership traits during prime-time hours. The issue data was used in preparing Table 1 for Chapter Five.

APPENDIX D

Measuring the Effects of the Mass Media on Voters

THE mass media's impact was determined by relating voters' exposure to various media channels during the 1972 general election to changes in their response to the candidates and issues. A description of how media exposure and voter change were measured and how these measures were systematically related is provided below.

Measuring Media Exposure

Television news: Exposure to the network evening news was measured by respondents' self-reports of their viewing. In both the early October and early November interviews, the respondents were given a viewing log that contained the network evening newscasts and were asked to indicate how often they had watched (see Figure 1). Additionally, respondents were asked several screening questions as a check on the accuracy of their reported news viewing.

Using the data obtained from the logs, an estimate was made of each respondent's exposure to network news during the 1972 general election. Respondents whose answers indicated they watched network news at least four nights per week were classified as "regular viewers" and those who watched less frequently were classified as "nonregular" viewers. Roughly half the respondents fell in each category, indicating that respondents overreported their network news exposure. To see if this overreporting affected the results

189

FIGURE 1. Log Used in Measuring Network Evening News Exposure

INSTRUCTIONS: Below is a list of television programs that are shown every weekday—Monday through Friday—in the early evening hours. These programs were shown 10 times in the last two weeks. Next to each program, please check the box that describes how many of the last 10 shows you personally watched.

TELEVISION SHOWS ON MONDAY THROUGH FRIDAY: EARLY EVENING (4 P.M.–8 P.M.)	Do not watch program	Watch program now and then but not in last 2 weeks	Of the last 10 shows, I watched:				
			1–2 Shows	3–4 Shows	5–6 Shows	7–8 Shows	9–10 Shows
BEFORE 6:00 P.M.							
Channel 3 Movie	( )	( )	( )	( )	( )	( )	( )
Ponderosa	( )	( )	( )	( )	( )	( )	( )
Star Trek	( )	( )	( )	( )	( )	( )	( )
6:00–6:30 P.M.							
Channel 3 Local News, Weather, Sports	( )	( )	( )	( )	( )	( )	( )
Channel 5 Local News, Weather, Sports	( )	( )	( )	( )	( )	( )	( )

Channel 9 Local News, Weather, Sports	( )		( )	( )	( )	( )	( )
6:30–7:00 P.M.							
The ABC Evening News: Smith and Reasoner (Channel 9)	( )	( )	( )	( )	( )	( )	( )
The CBS Evening News: Cronkite (Channel 5)	( )	( )	( )	( )	( )	( )	( )
The NBC Evening News: Chancellor and Brinkley (Channel 3)	( )	( )	( )	( )	( )	( )	( )
AFTER 7:00 P.M.							
To Tell the Truth	( )	( )	( )	( )	( )	( )	( )
Merv Griffin	( )	( )	( )	( )	( )	( )	( )
Truth or Consequences							

presented in this book, a more restrictive definition of "regular viewers" was constructed. On this measure thirty-four percent fell into the high exposure category. Analyses with the more restrictive measure, however, yielded the same results as analyses with the first measure.

Newspapers: Newspaper exposure was measured by an index created from the frequency with which people said they read the daily newspaper and the frequency with which they claimed to read specific newspaper sections. In both the early October and early November interviews, the respondents were asked, "During the past seven days, about how many days did you get a chance to read the newspaper?" In the November interview only, respondents were asked to indicate on the form below how much attention they gave to various sections of the newspaper. People's exposure to these newspaper sections was measured because television *news* exposure was determined by people's viewing of specific television

	Do not read section	Read section now and then but not regularly	Read section most days but just skim it	Read section most days and read it closely
Business and financial section	☐	☐	☐	☐
Editorial and opinion section	☐	☐	☐	☐
Women's section	☐	☐	☐	☐
Sports section	☐	☐	☐	☐
Front pages	☐	☐	☐	☐
Comic section	☐	☐	☐	☐
Local news section	☐	☐	☐	☐

programming, and not by their level of television viewing in general. Consequently, newspaper *news* exposure should also be specific to content. In addition, in each interview, respondents were asked several screening questions as a check on the accuracy of these responses.

From these data sources, an estimate was made of each respondent's exposure to the newspaper's political content during the 1972 general election. Respondents who reported reading the newspaper an average of six days per week and who also indicated paying at least moderate attention to the paper's news sections (front pages, editorial pages, local news pages) were classified as "regular newspaper readers." All other respondents were classified as "nonregular newspaper readers." This procedure placed 54 percent of the respondents in the high newspaper exposure category and 46 percent in the low exposure category. As with network news, these figures suggest that respondents overreported their newspaper exposure. An analysis was then conducted using a more restrictive categorization of high newspaper exposure (only the top 32 percent in reported exposure ended up in the high category). No significant differences from the book's findings occurred when using the more restrictive categorization.

Televised political advertising: Exposure to the candidates' televised spots was measured using program-by-program logs to estimate the amount of time each respondent spent viewing television between the hours of 7 and 11 P.M., the period during which most political spots were aired. The logs were administered in both the October and November interviews (see Figure 2). Again, screening questions also were asked respondents as a check on their replies.

Respondents who reported watching television about one hour or less on an average evening were placed in the low exposure category and those viewing more than about an hour were placed in the high exposure category. Using this procedure 69 percent of respondents fell in the high advertising exposure category and 31 percent in the low category.

FIGURE 2. Log Used in Measuring People's Exposure to Televised Political Advertising

INSTRUCTIONS: Below is a list of nighttime television programs that are shown in this area once a week. You are to indicate *your own viewing* of each of these programs during the past four weeks. If you never watch the program, check the first box. If you watch the program now and then, but have not watched it in the last four weeks, check the next box. Finally, if you have actually watched the program in the *last four weeks*, then check the box that tells how many of the last four shows you have watched.

NIGHTTIME TELEVISION SHOWS	Do not watch program	Watch program now and then but not in last 4 weeks	In last 4 weeks I watched			
			1 Show	2 Shows	3 Shows	4 Shows
MONDAY NIGHT						
Young Dr. Kildare	⌣	⌣	⌣	⌣	⌣	⌣
Let's Make a Deal	⌣	⌣	⌣	⌣	⌣	⌣
Rowan and Martin's Laugh-In	⌣	⌣	⌣	⌣	⌣	⌣
Gunsmoke	⌣	⌣	⌣	⌣	⌣	⌣
The Rookies	⌣	⌣	⌣	⌣	⌣	⌣
NBC Monday Night Movie	⌣	⌣	⌣	⌣	⌣	⌣
Here's Lucy	⌣	⌣	⌣	⌣	⌣	⌣
NFL Monday Night Football	⌣	⌣	⌣	⌣	⌣	⌣
The Doris Day Show	⌣	⌣	⌣	⌣	⌣	⌣
The Bill Cosby Show	⌣	⌣	⌣	⌣	⌣	⌣

TUESDAY NIGHT

Untamed World

I've Got a Secret

Bonanza

Cousin Maude

NOTE: Log administered to respondents included all seven evenings of the week.

Measuring Voters' Issue Awareness and Candidate Images

Issues: Issue awareness was measured by having respondents indicate the certainty with which they believed Nixon and McGovern held a position on key election issues. People indicated their beliefs by responding to seven-point scales such as the following:

George McGovern favors spending less money
on the military

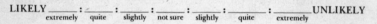

LIKELY ____ : ____ : ____ : ____ : ____ : ____ : ____ UNLIKELY
extremely quite slightly not sure slightly quite extremely

Respondents marked these scales during both the initial interview in September and the final preelection interview in November. Since respondents indicated their issue beliefs in both September and November, it was possible to determine whether their awareness of a candidate's issue stand increased, stayed the same, or decreased during the general election. Consider, for example, voters' responses to the above scale. George McGovern's actual position was that he favored reducing military spending. Now, if between September and November, a respondent's belief about McGovern's military spending stand moved toward the LIKELY end of the scale, his awareness of McGovern's stand improved. If he marked the same point in both September and November, his issue awareness stayed the same. And finally, if his belief moved toward the UNLIKELY end of the scale, his issue awareness of McGovern's military spending stand decreased.

When issue change is shown in the chapters, the percentages were determined from how various respondents (for example, those who regularly watched the evening news) changed their positions on the scales. The following formula was used in calculating these percentages. It provides a measure of whether more people change toward increased issue awareness or more changed toward decreased awareness:

$$\text{Percentage} = \frac{\begin{array}{c}\text{Number of voters}\\\text{increasing their}\\\text{issue awareness}\end{array} - \begin{array}{c}\text{Number of voters}\\\text{decreasing their}\\\text{issue awareness}\end{array}}{\begin{array}{c}\text{Number of voters}\\\text{increasing their}\\\text{issue awareness}\end{array} + \begin{array}{c}\text{Number of voters}\\\text{decreasing their}\\\text{issue awareness}\end{array}} \times 100$$

When this formula is used, a positive number (e.g., 24 percent) always results when more people gain in issue awareness than lose. A negative number (e.g., -16 percent) always results when more people decrease in issue awareness. Finally, the larger the absolute number, the more overwhelmingly people are changing toward increased or decreased issue awareness. In the text, precise terms are used when referring to the percentages resulting from use of the formula. *Percent increase* (e.g., "there was a 35 percent increase in issue information") is used to express the situation where more people gained in issue awareness than lost. *Percent decrease* (e.g., "there was a 20 percent decrease in issue information") is used to express the situation where more people lost than gained.

Images: People's images of the candidates were measured by having respondents indicate the certainty with which they felt Nixon and McGovern possessed or lacked various personal and leadership traits. People indicated their beliefs by marking seven-point scales such as this one:

Richard Nixon is trustworthy as a person

LIKELY _____ : _____ : _____ : _____ : _____ : _____ : _____ UNLIKELY
    extremely quite   slightly not sure slightly quite extremely

Respondents marked these scales during both the initial September interview and the November preelection interview. As with issue awareness, it was thus possible to determine how their images of the candidates changed. In the above example, if a respondent moved toward the LIKELY end of the scale between the two interviews, his image of Nixon improved. If he moved toward the UNLIKELY end, Nixon's image deteriorated. A formula similar to the issue formula was used to assess what image changes occurred in the various groups shown in the chapter tables. A positive number indicates that more people's image of the candidate improved and a negative one that more people's image became worse. In the text, *percent improvement* (e.g., "McGovern's image had a 25 percent improvement") is used to express situations where more people's image of the candidate improved, and *percent decline* (e.g., "McGovern's image had a 30 percent decline") is used to express situations where more people's image of a candidate declined.

Estimating Media Impact

Estimates of the media's influence on people were obtained by relating respondents' media exposure to changes in their issue awareness and images. The assumption was that, if a given media channel was having an influence on people's issue awareness or their images, regular users of that channel should have had changes consistent with that influence, changes which were not evident in nonusers. For example, if televised political advertising was informing people about the issues, those respondents exposed to many ads should have had a greater increase in their issue awareness than people who did not see many ads.

An example will clarify the entire procedure. One of the issues covered by political advertising was McGovern's intention to reduce military spending. Using the formula discussed above, the percentage for people who saw many ads was 66 percent. For people who saw few ads, the percentage was 45 percent. Obviously, advertising exposure was related to increased issue awareness. Of course, it was the pattern of change on several issues, rather than a single issue, that was the basis for the book's conclusions.

In examining the media's impact on issue awareness, news

channels (television news and the newspaper) were assessed somewhat differently than televised political advertising. The operating assumption for news channels is that they have a journalistic responsibility for informing the voters. Consequently, their impact was examined across the full range of election issues even though, as the case with network news, a news medium may have given little or no coverage to certain of the issues. This provides an estimate of their total contribution to an informed electorate. With political advertising, its effects were examined only on those issues which were contained in commercials. Advertising is limited to those issues that a candidate feels will advantage his campaign, and it makes sense to look for effects only on these issues. This provides an estimate of whether the candidates' issue messages are having an effect on voters.

The analysis of political advertising effects produced a finding that will be informative to communication researchers. Often, media effects research has paid little attention to media content and has simply correlated media exposure with people's political opinions and knowledge. But this study points out the need for considering media content. A *positive* association was found between advertising exposure and people's awareness on issues *covered* by advertising. On those issues *not covered* in the candidates' commercials, however, there was a *negative* association between advertising exposure and issue awareness. If content had not been considered, this study would have reached an inappropriate conclusion. Advertising's effects on those issues it covered would have been cancelled by those issues it did not cover, and the conclusion would have been that advertising had no influence. Careful assessments of the media's audience impact clearly require an accounting of media content.

APPENDIX E

Statistical Significance of Key Relationships

REPRODUCED in this appendix are tables containing the statistical significance of the key relationships presented in the book. The tables are based on standard difference of means tests. The means in each of the categories were based on changes on the seven-point scales between the start and end of the general election campaign.

Table 1. The Impact of Network News Exposure on People's Issue Awareness During 1972 General Election (Reproduction of Table 1 in Chapter Two)

	Mean change for nonregular viewers	Mean change for regular viewers	1-tail probability
Nixon policies:			
Vietnam war	.128	−.069	wd
Government spending	.190	−.080	wd
Military spending	.356	.495	.178
Busing	.463	.378	wd
China	.240	.179	wd
Russia	.164	.188	.402
Foreign commitments	.157	.150	wd
Taxes on upper incomes	.172	−.007	wd
Law and order	−.071	−.083	wd
Jobs for the unemployed	.183	.249	.330
Amnesty	.447	.562	.199
Drugs	.118	.066	wd
McGovern policies:			
Military spending	.661	.585	wd
Vietnam withdrawal	.218	.304	.240
Amnesty	.322	.258	wd
Political corruption	−.046	.052	.234
Taxes on upper incomes	.099	.370	.025
Jobs for the unemployed	.666	.462	wd
Average on all issues	.265	.233	wd

The working hypothesis is that network news exposure does increase issue awareness. The 1-tail probability is based on the hypothesis. When the mean change for nonregular viewers is greater, the relationship is marked wd.

TABLE 2. The Impact of Newspaper Reading on People's Issue Awareness During 1972 General Election (Reproduction of Table 2 in Chapter Two)

	Mean change for nonregular readers	Mean change for regular readers	1-tail prob- ability
Nixon policies:			
Vietnam war	−.106	.113	.043
Government spending	.029	.083	.353
Military spending	.266	.535	.037
Busing	.351	.515	.129
China	.095	.283	.024
Russia	.070	.250	.032
Foreign commitments	.048	.238	.018
Taxes on upper incomes	.103	.064	wd
Law and order	−.133	−.041	.177
Jobs for the unemployed	.096	.338	.054
Amnesty	.451	.589	.151
Drugs	−.004	.179	.074
McGovern policies:			
Military spending	.449	.753	.018
Vietnam withdrawal	.172	.331	.098
Amnesty	.252	.347	.230
Political corruption	−.040	.127	.103
Taxes on upper incomes	.158	.303	.150
Jobs for the unemployed	.654	.465	wd
Average on all issues	.195	.299	.009

The working hypothesis is that newspaper exposure does increase issue awareness. The 1-tail probability is based on the hypothesis.

TABLE 3. The Impact of Network News Exposure on People's Images of Nixon and McGovern During 1972 General Election

	A	B	C	D
Nixon's Image				
Experienced	wd	.028	.045	.188
Forward-looking	.227	.045	.741	.610
Confidence-inspiring	.044	.005	.876	.793
Trustworthy	.001	.016	.541	.083
Appealing	.005	.004	.155	.691
Compassionate	.006	.356	.832	.060
Not "political"	.177	.006	.342	.607
Average change	.001	.001	.316	.646
McGovern's Image				
Experienced	.092	.001	.095	.237
Forward-looking	.005	.079	.518	.670
Confidence-inspiring	.080	.001	.551	.006
Trustworthy	.001	.001	.244	.625
Appealing	.082	.043	.825	.408
Compassionate	.179	.170	.827	.926
Not "political"	.003	.001	.143	.055
Average change	.001	.001	.960	.098

Table includes only significance levels for difference in means. Significance levels are for the following: (A) Difference between means for Nixon-oriented regular network news viewers and McGovern-oriented regular network news viewers; (B) Difference between means for Nixon-oriented nonregular network news viewers and McGovern-oriented nonregular network news viewers; (C) Difference between means for Nixon-oriented regular viewers and Nixon-oriented nonregular viewers; (D) Difference between means for McGovern-oriented regular viewers and McGovern-oriented nonregular viewers. The working hypothesis for both

A and B is that images will change in accord with people's political orientations. A 1-tail probability based on that hypothesis is provided for both A and B. The working hypothesis for C and D is that television exposure affects voters' images but that the direction of image change (whether the candidate's image improves or deteriorates) is not predictable. A 2-tail probability based on that hypothesis is provided for both C and D.

TABLE 4. The Impact of Political Advertising Exposure on People's Images of Nixon and McGovern During 1972 General Election (Reproduction of Table 1 in Chapter Six)

	A	B	C	D
Nixon's Image				
Experienced	.461	.233	.147	.990
Forward-looking	.335	.016	.222	.297
Confidence-inspiring	.061	.003	.199	.054
Trustworthy	.001	.001	.769	.709
Appealing	.002	.056	.576	.802
Compassionate	.062	.036	.363	.890
Not "political"	.017	.162	.835	.437
Average change	.001	.001	.699	.507
McGovern's Image				
Experienced	.001	wd	.112	.016
Forward-looking	.002	.091	.720	.048
Confidence-inspiring	.014	.009	.711	.667
Trustworthy	.001	.003	.682	.653
Appealing	.059	.029	.348	.691
Compassionate	.165	.131	.736	.811
Not "political"	.002	.001	.739	.223
Average change	.001	.001	.997	.427

Table includes only significance levels for difference in means. Significance levels are for the following: (A) Difference between means for Nixon-oriented high advertising viewers and McGovern-oriented high advertising viewers; (B) Difference between means for Nixon-oriented low advertising viewers and McGovern-oriented low advertising viewers; (C) Difference between means for Nixon-oriented high advertising viewers and Nixon-oriented low advertising viewers; (D) Difference between means for McGovern-oriented high advertising viewers and McGovern-oriented low advertising viewers. The working hypothesis for both A and

B is that images will change in accord with people's political orientations. A 1-tail probability based on that hypothesis is provided for both A and B. The working hypothesis for C and D is that television exposure affects voters' images but that the direction of image change (whether the candidate's image improves or deteriorates) is not predictable. A 2-tail probability based on that hypothesis is provided for both C and D.

Table 5. The Impact of Political Advertising Exposure on People's Issue Awareness During 1972 General Election (Reproduction of Table 2 in Chapter Six)

	Exposed to few spots	Exposed to many spots	1-tail probability
Nixon's China policy	.071	.267	.026
Nixon's Russia policy	.098	.217	.107
McGovern's military spending position	.363	.734	.009
Nixon's military spending position	.309	.465	.153
McGovern's tax policy	.170	.259	.278
Nixon's stance toward political corruption	.196	.132	wd
Nixon's Vietnam policy	.005	−.037	wd
McGovern's stand on Vietnam withdrawal	.236	.263	.417
Nixon's policy on foreign commitments	.068	.170	.135
Average on all issues	.173	.275	.020

The working hypothesis is that political advertising exposure does increase issue awareness. The 1-tail probability is based on the hypothesis.

APPENDIX F

Chronicle of One Television Network's Campaign Coverage During the Last Month of the 1972 Election

CHAPTER One presented a log of one network's election coverage during the final five weekdays (October 31 through November 6) of the 1972 campaign. Described below are all the campaign stories that appeared on that network during the last *month* of the election.

Monday, October 9
Nixon spent this Columbus Day in the White House, while Pat Nixon attended parade in Chicago. (0:17)
McGovern marched in New York City's Columbus Day Parade. Rockefeller said McGovern did it for political purposes and was asked not to march by parade officials. McGovern said he was invited and the crowd was quite friendly to him. This was his first stop in a crucial two-week tour to close the gap with Nixon. (2:33)

Tuesday, October 10
White House refused to comment on Watergate-Segretti matter. McGovern said that if anything like this had happened with his staff, he would have been held responsible, but he said nobody blames Nixon. (1:25)
McGovern went to Chicago today where things were "looking up." McGovern and Mayor Daley united in leading an

effort to get voters registered and out to vote Democratic. (3:35)

Harris poll showed a very slight gain of one percent for McGovern though he still trailed 60 percent to 33 percent with 7 percent undecided. (0:20)

Wednesday, October 11
No evening newscast: preempted by sporting event.

Thursday, October 12
Nixon flew to Atlanta. Big event was huge motorcade through the city. There was a shouting match between anti-war demonstrators and Nixon supporters. In speech, Nixon appealed for Southerners to drop traditional Democratic allegiance. (2:08)

Commentary on how the Atlanta campaign visit demonstrated that Nixon campaign was Nixon's and not the Republican party's. (1:09)

Report on how the South has changed politically. Before the South was solidly Democratic, but now the South is Nixon Country. Local Democratic candidates avoid McGovern backers and local Republican candidates try to tie themselves to Nixon. (2:44)

McGovern said he would choose a former Johnson official who had attempted to scale down the war as Secretary of Defense. (0:28)

Friday, October 13
In Seattle, McGovern outlined an Ethics in Government Program that proposed a limit on campaign contributions. McGovern attacked Nixon's association with "big money." (2:34)

Eleanor McGovern was admitted to the hospital for tests after eight straight days of campaigning. Doctors said it was not serious, but she will stay for another day. (0:16)

Pravda reported a vast majority of American experts predict a Nixon victory. Pravda attributed this to Nixon's improved relations with the Soviets. (0:22)

Monday, October 16
Nixon unexpectedly turned up to speak to the families of POW's. He spoke of the negotiations and blasted McGovern's Vietnam and amnesty stands. (2:45)

McGregor (Nixon's campaign chairman) said McGovern and his confederates are losing and getting desperate. (0:46)

McGovern charged Nixon staff employed more than fifty people to infiltrate Democratic campaigns and bring disarray and confusion to Democratic ranks. (0:47)

The Gallup poll showed slight improvement for McGovern but Nixon remained far ahead. (0:23)

Shriver, in New England, found encouragement in polls. Shriver saw exodus from Nixon ranks. Many in campaign, however, are resigned to defeat. (1:51)

Tuesday, October 17
John Connally, Shriver, and McGovern commented on Watergate. (0:41)

McGovern was in Texas today. For two days, McGovern had been appearing before very large enthusiastic crowds here. Although the polls still showed him far behind Nixon, his receptions have increased his belief that he will win here. If crowds were any indication, the McGovern campaign could be catching fire just as Humphrey campaign did in 1968.(2:13)

Commentary on differences between the Humphrey campaign and McGovern's. (1:47)

Connally said he might leave the Democratic Party permanently if it continues under the leadership of McGovern. (0:10)

Wednesday , October 18
Nixon to give paid political radio talk. (0:08)

McGovern challenged Nixon to a televised debate and said he will even pay for the time. (0:07)

POW Organization endorsed Nixon candidacy. (0:05)

Florida AFL-CIO endorsed McGovern's candidacy. (0:06)

Thursday, October 19

Commentary on campaign getting more personal as corruption becomes a bigger issue. (0:14)

Harris poll showed citizens have been following Watergate but that two out of three don't believe Nixon was in any way involved. (0:16)

McGovern, campaigning in Pennsylvania and Ohio, said, "Nixon is up to his ears in political sabotage." He further said that the Nixon administration was the most corrupt in history. (1:45)

Agnew in Connecticut dismissed corruption charges with a joke and dismissed McGovern in same way. (0:20)

Eleanor McGovern was described as dead tired and will rest at home rather than campaign. (0:12)

White House said Nixon will make two more radio talks this weekend and motorcade through part of Ohio next weekend. (0:08)

Friday, October 20

Nixon traveled to Philadelphia to sign revenue-sharing bill. A crowd of antiwar demonstrators gathered outside Independence Square while the crowd inside (admitted by invitation only) listened to Nixon's speech. Despite tight security, his speech was disrupted by an antiwar demonstrator. The bill Nixon signed will give thirty billion dollars to states and cities over the next five years. (2:35)

McGovern to give television address tonight. In an interview today, McGovern spoke hopefully, and said he thinks things are beginning to move in his campaign. (2:35)

Palo Alto County in Iowa has voted for the winning candidate ever since 1896. Straw polls there produce conflicting results. (3:11)

Monday, October 23

Nixon motorcaded through suburbs of New York City and had a very enthusiastic turnout. Advance work was quite good. Dissenters greatly outnumbered by Nixon supporters. (2:05)

McGovern was in Philadelphia to begin his fourth campaign swing across the nation. He said he thinks things are picking up. He spoke to veterans in the VA hospital. McGovern plans to spend most of the week preparing his television material.(2:00)

Agnew charged that Sargent Shriver was running a cosmetic campaign that did not inspire confidence. (0:15)

Shriver was in Ohio talking about the peace movement. He said Nixon had been driven to peace by the McGovern-Shriver campaign. (0:20)

A report on how some southern Wisconsin farmers felt about campaign. (2:48)

Tuesday, October 24

McGovern, in Ohio, said peace was not achieved four years ago on the same terms discussed now because President Nixon wanted to avoid criticism from right-wing hawks. (0:32)

Agnew, campaigning in Utah, spoke at Brigham Young University. He spoke in very general terms about Vietnam and did not mention anything about the state of negotiations. (1:30)

In Chicago, Mayor Daley staged a parade for Shriver. The crowd was disappointingly small and unenthusiastic. Shriver had an argument with one spectator. After the parade, Shriver attended a meeting with Daley and his precinct workers. After some initial misgivings, Daley's organization appeared to be working hard for McGovern. (2:00)

Transportation Secretary Volpe and Nixon's daughter, Tricia, were in West Virginia for the dedication of a new transit system, but it was more like a political rally. Volpe and antiwar demonstrators had a verbal clash. (2:33)

Wednesday, October 25

McGovern made a statement based on Washington *Post* stories indicating that corruption would be the dominant theme for the rest of the campaign. McGovern said that Watergate could be traced right to Haldeman and that it was squarely in Nixon's lap. (1:47)

McGovern to make a TV broadcast tonight. Nixon made a radio talk earlier. (0:30)

Thursday, October 26

McGovern made a statement on peace settlement. He said it could have been done four years ago, but he would give his support now to any effort that would lead to peace. (1:42)

McGovern, in Iowa City, urged Nixon not to let Saigon block the agreement worked out between U.S. and Hanoi. (0:09)

Nixon flew to Appalachia for two campaign appearances. (0:16)

In South Carolina, Shriver said peace agreement is a triumph but that it could have happened four years ago. (0:13)

Kennedy told reporters in Chicago that Nixon will obviously benefit if peace comes before the election. (0:08)

Friday, October 27

Nixon made another radio talk. (0:15)

McGovern campaigned in Los Angeles. He revealed a secret Nixon report on how to undercut the labor movement. Ted Kennedy came to California rallies because McGovern felt he had strength in California. (1:50)

Pollster Sam Lubell said Vietnam peace might hurt Nixon, but not seriously. (0:23)

Agnew said he will not talk about Vietnam in his campaign appearances. (0:16)

Report on campaign in Texas revealed Nixon is quite strong, though it has always been strongly Democratic. A street poll showed what real polls show—Nixon's ahead.

McGovern is strong in universities but only slightly. It looks like Nixon has Texas sewn up. (2:09)

Monday, Oct. 30

In Connecticut, McGovern called Nixon Mr. Veto. He criticized Nixon's domestic record. McGovern said he is better able to deal with social and economic problems than Nixon. This will probably be his last campaign appearance in a small state. From now on, he must go to the states with the most electoral votes. (1:54)

A special report on Ohio. Ohio has been slightly Republican in its presidential voting. Nixon is quite strong in conservative southern Ohio, and McGovern is being hurt by labor union neutrality in the northern areas. Both candidates have emphasized Ohio, but Nixon appears in best position. (2:13)

Tuesday, October 31

The latest Harris Poll shows Nixon has slightly increased his lead over McGovern to 28 percent. (0:29)

McGovern appears to be doing well with the young as reflected in his crowds, but the polls indicate that overall he is not doing that well. McGovern's people believe the polls are wrong and he can win. (0:87)

Pennsylvania is an important state to McGovern. The eastern part of the state is Nixon country. Appalachian Pennsylvania usually supports the Democrats, particularly in the cities. McGovern may be seriously hurt by withholding of union support in Pittsburgh and low registration of black voters. Both candidates have campaigned frequently here, but it looks like McGovern will need a lot more help if he is to carry the state. (2:05)

Nixon to go on television for first paid political speech of his campaign. He will start to pick up the pace of his campaign in this last week. (0:25)

Wednesday, November 1

Nixon in a radio address said he is doing more for the

cities than Johnson did. McGovern said the Democratic Congress deserves the credit. (0:27)

McGovern had a noontime parade through New York City. He was out to attract the ethnic vote and gave a rally in the garment district. A huge crowd assembled to hear McGovern attack Nixon's handling of the economy and Ted Kennedy saying he thought McGovern would come from behind. McGovern cancelled a speech in Minnesota because of a sore throat but flew to Chicago to speak tonight. (2:00)

Shriver campaigned in Portland and Seattle today. (0:07)

Agnew ran into a group of hecklers in San Diego. Agnew told demonstrators that since they use fascist tactics they ought to wear brown shirts. Agnew went on to say McGovernism will become an obscure footnote in history. (1:59)

Analysis of Democratic California shows that many Democrats will jump to Nixon. McGovern canvassing is trying to reverse polls that have Nixon leading in the state. Nixon people are working just to get their voters to the polls. (2:17)

Commentary on how Nixon has hardly campaigned and still is far ahead in the polls while McGovern has campaigned frantically. It appears that the electorate cares very little about this election. (0:74)

Thursday, November 2
Mrs. Nixon was heckled in Boston today, and Agnew was heckled yesterday in San Diego. The Nixon people blame McGovern people and, the McGovern people said it was a "put-up job" by the GOP. (0:27)

McGovern attended huge rally at the University of Cincinnati. McGovern was heckled by a group of Nixon supporters. McGovern charged that the Agnew hecklers in San Diego had been planted to disrupt McGovern's campaign efforts. Despite the likelihood of Cincinnati going Republican, McGovern's staff people think they have a shot at carrying Ohio. (1:55)

Klein (Nixon's Communication Director) said he thought

Nixon would carry at least forty-five of the fifty states in the election. (0:17)

McGovern must carry Michigan if he is to have any chance to win. The only important issue to Michigan voters is busing. Wallace's success in the Democratic Party primary illustrates the fact. Most Michigan voters feel Nixon will do what he can to stop busing while McGovern would not. Michigan seems in the Nixon column. (2:20)

Gallup Poll showed that one big area where McGovern lacks support is among blue-collar workers. He is receiving less support among this segment of the public than any Democrat since 1936. (0:26)

Thursday, November 2

In a traditionally Democratic section of Cleveland, workers claimed they would vote for Nixon by a large margin. Over the last six weeks Nixon's support has slightly eroded but still heavily Nixon. (3:47)

Commentary on how ugly recent history must be considered in analyzing why America votes as it does. Search for order and calmness might explain 1972 election results. (2:25)

Friday, November 3

McGovern speaking in Michigan said he is skeptical that peace will come soon. He then went to tape a televised talk for tonight. He is to say that Nixon is deceiving the people. (1:56)

Nixon made his only campaign appearance in Illinois. He fully expects to win Illinois this year. He ignored hecklers and said he wanted peace with honor. He then went to Oklahoma and Rhode Island to help local Republicans. (1:59)

Illinois is an important state for a candidate. Chicago is heavily Democratic and its suburbs are Republican. Southern Illinois is largely Republican with pockets of Democratic strength. As a result, Illinois is fairly evenly divided. Nixon has a lead, but McGovern appears to be on the move according to polls. (2:18)

In Wyoming, Agnew attended an overwhelmingly favorable rally, but his speech was disrupted by a small group of protestors. He accused McGovern of unprecedented meddling in foreign policy. In Denver, Agnew was again heckled. (2:13)

Shriver attacked Nixon's delay in signing the Paris agreement. He said voters might be swayed if they believe Nixon is letting Thieu block peace efforts. (2:17)

From April 8 to October 26 McGovern committees spent eighteen million dollars. During this same period, Nixon committees spent twice as much. Nixon people spent even more when those funds not reported are included. Campaign spending is skyrocketing. (0:57)

Monday, November 6
McGovern's last day of campaigning took him from New York City to California and then to South Dakota by the end of the day. He said Nixon has deceived the people on peace. He campaigned to huge crowds in Philadelphia at noon. McGovern reflected on campaign and said he would not run again in 1976 if he lost. (1:51)

Nixon's only campaign act on this last campaign day was to tape a televised statement. Nixon's campaign appearances have been very minimal and he seems confident of victory. (1:31)

Shriver's strategy for the last day of the campaign was to appear in as many places as possible. He visited five key states in the day. He started in Pittsburgh and then held a press conference in Cleveland. (1:45)

Agnew appeared superconfident in Philadelphia. Protestors were restrained. He spoke at the Fraternal Order of Police. He then went to Virginia to campaign for a senatorial candidate. (1:51)

Commentary on tremendous amount of money thrown into campaign and how most money still comes from big contributors. (1:53)

The polls show the likelihood of a Nixon landslide. The

Gallup Poll showed McGovern trailing by 26 percent. This is the second biggest lead any incumbent has had since the polls began. (0:35)

Commentary that the 1972 election will probably be remembered as the campaign in which the President campaigned so little. It seems analogous to the 1944 Roosevelt campaign in which FDR hardly campaigned. It seems the voters suffered from the lack of the campaign. (0:61)